EXECUTIVE Guide to
Speech-Driven Computer Systems

Springer-Verlag London Ltd.

Malcolm McPherson

EXECUTIVE
Guide to

Speech-Driven Computer Systems

Springer

Malcolm McPherson, BSc
Shakespeare SpeechWriter UK Ltd
Constitutional Buildings
High Street
East Grinstead
West Sussex
RH19 3AW

British Library Cataloguing in Publication Data
McPherson, Malcolm
   Executive Guide to Speech-driven
   Computer Systems – (Executive Guides)
   I. Title II. Series
   006.454
   ISBN 978-3-540-19911-3   ISBN 978-1-4471-0385-1 (eBook)
   DOI 10.1007/978-1-4471-0385-1

Library of Congress Cataloging-in-Publication Data
A catalog record for this book is available from the Library of Congress

Originally published by Springer-Verlag London Limited in 1995

This book was dictated using OfficeSpeak® (product by Shakespeare SpeechWriter)

Typeset by Richard Powell Editorial and Production Services, Basingstoke, Hants RG22 4TX
34/3830 543210   (Printed on acid-free paper)

Contents

Preface

Since the 1950s it has been the dream of man to be able to give verbal instructions to a robot or man machine. Early science fiction films depict the hero talking to a computer.

In 1952 Captain Kirk can be seen talking to the main control computer.

In 1968 the film *2001* depicted the hero conversing with the space station computer named HAL.

In 1974 the film *The Blade Runner* depicted the hero controlling a computer by speech to analyse a small fragment.

In the 1980s, both in America and in Europe, governments and large corporations spent millions trying to overcome the technical difficulties of communicating with a computer by speech.

In its heyday IBM Corporation allocated a sizeable budget to researching speech activation. This research during the 1980s did not really produce any saleable products. It was a breakaway group led by Dr Janet Baker in the late 1980s that produced the first widely sold commercial product.

In the early 1990s Dr Baker's company, Dragon Systems, Inc. of Massachusetts, launched its large vocabulary product *Dragon Dictate* on the DOS platform.

These developments set the scene for an explosion of speech products, which are now just hitting the market.

Large corporations like Philips are launching products, the multi-billion Japanese keyboard manufacturers ALPS is launching a speech product, and smaller development companies like Shakespeare, Kurzweil, Learnhaurt and Haustie and Scott are all launching products. Even IBM, early in 1994, made a comeback and launched their own Personal Dictation System.

Every business, every company, every manager, every executive must be aware that the speech activation of computers is going to radically change how people work in the future.

The next five years may signal the demise of the keyboard as we know it.

With this scenario in mind, the *Executive Guide to Speech-Driven Computers*, which is part of the Springer Executive Guide Series, has been written to give directors, executives and managers an insight into what speech activation is all about and to give them enough understandable data to make decisions in implementing this new technology in their businesses or companies.

In writing this book I am indebted to Professor Richard Ennals and the Dean of Kingston Business School, Professor David Miles. Not only did they support speech activation when it was in its embryo stage and not only did they ensure that Kingston University was the first university to install a speech laboratory, but also it was their enthusiasm that cajoled me into sitting down and "speaking" this book.

I am also grateful for the support I have received from my staff at Shakespeare SpeechWriter. They have had to put up with the excuse that I am not there because I am "writing my book".

Especially, I would like to acknowledge the help that I have had from Jan Metzger (Development Director of Shakespeare SpeechWriter), who is probably the most enthusiastic person in the world when discussing any topic with a high-tech or economics flavour. His brilliance has contributed to the section on artificial intelligence and neural networks. It was in these subjects that he graduated with first class honours at Sussex University, and I feel sure that this will not be the last time that we see Jan's name in print.

Lastly, I have written this book from a completely practical and pragmatic point of view. I am not trying to impress the academics in any shape or form. I have written it from one executive to another, in what I hope is very understandable language. I am grateful for the support of Kingston University and the Series Editors in particular chapters, and in the compilation of the additional notes.

Malcolm McPherson
MD Shakespeare SpeechWriter
July 1995

Series Editor's Introduction

Executive Guide to Speech-Driven Computers is one of the first titles in the Springer Executive Guides series, which is concerned with managing in the context of new and emerging technology.

At a time when all managers are becoming accustomed to grappling with keyboards and personal computer screens, we are offered the alluring prospect of talking to the computer. As a research objective this is not new: however, the technology now works, and the first generation of commercial products are now both available and affordable. How can they be used to business advantage at a time of unprecedented change?

This book, and the experience of the companies on which it is based, demonstrates that successful diffusion and adoption depends on more than technical feasibility. The spread of technology requires the enthusiastic support of people and organisations, based on the success of niche applications.

Rather than offering a detached account of the efforts of others, the book is itself an example of the application of the technology. The text has been dictated to the computer, using one of the systems described. The resulting text is a new form of product: the medium is at least part of the message.

The power of speech has long been understood by playwrights, such as William Shakespeare, and demonstrated on the stage. Othello was conscious of how his speech was regarded in Venetian high society:

> *"Rude am I in my speech*
> *And little bless'd with the soft phrase of peace"*

Othello I. iii. 81

Hamlet sought to outwit and unmask his murderous uncle Claudius by adding his own speech to a play to be performed by visiting actors. The speech would have to be delivered in a particular way:

> *"Speak the speech, I pray you, as I pronounced it to you, trippingly on the tongue"*
>
> *Hamlet* III. ii. 1

Great effort can be involved in preparing a speech for a major occasion, as was admitted by Sir Andrew Ague-Cheek to Sir Toby Belch in *Twelfth Night:*

> *"I would be loath to cast away my speech, for besides that it is excellently well penned, I have taken great pains to con it."*
>
> *Twelfth Night* I. v. 184

Speech is not merely used for description, but can be an action, for example inflaming the emotions of others. Mark Antony declared, in *Julius Caesar:*

> *"For I have neither wit, nor words, nor worth, Action, nor utterance, nor power of speech, To stir men's blood; I only speak right on; I tell you that which you yourselves do know."*
>
> *Julius Caesar* III. ii. 220

The author Malcolm McPherson is Managing Director of Shakespeare SpeechWriter Ltd, one of the major manufacturers and vendors of a range of speech-activated products. His primary concern is for the business user, and he introduces a variety of technologies and products that offer practical benefits. The book is a practical account from a pioneering small company, seeking to transfer advanced technology to the commercial market.

At the end of each chapter there are some general comments and questions by the series editor for the reader to consider. The intention of the author and the series editor is to persuade the reader to reflect on current practice, and explore the application of these new ideas and experiences to the practical circumstances of the reader's own organization.

A concluding Appendix by the series editor considers the practically orientated account by the author in the context of research, technology transfer and the future direction of business. We offer straightforward answers to the following questions:

- Why is speech technology important?
- Why is it important for busy executives today?
- How will speech technology affect the executive and the organization?
- How can speech technology offer competitive advantage?
- What are the next steps?

Richard Ennals
Kingston Business School
Kingston University
May 1995

Introduction

The Speech-Activation Market

Two years ago anyone analysing the speech-activation market would have come to the conclusion that it was an extremely minor niche part of the computer industry, geared to catering for users with a major mobility disability. Then, there were probably not more than 1000 speech-activation systems in use worldwide. A very large percentage of these would have been installed in the disabled market.

The disabled market was an obvious target for speech activation, because users in this category have nowhere else to turn in order to become productive. Later in this book we will review one case history that exemplifies why operating a computer solely by voice is such a lifesaver for the permanently disabled.

During 1994 the reliance on this segment of the market changed. The computer exhibition held in the autumn at Olympia sported no fewer than 10 different stands demonstrating voice as a new major feature.

What has happened in such a short space of time to suddenly make this new technology appeal to a much wider audience?

The Two-Finger Factor

The first factor lies in a set of very simple statistics. The average touch typist can type on a keyboard at a rate of between 40 and 70 words per minute. The top professional typist could probably manage 90–100 words per minute, but operators with that sort of skill are very few and far between.

The normal computer user who has had to learn to use the computer and type his or her own letters, usually with two fingers, types at a rate of between 5 and 25 words a minute: 95% of all computer users are *not* touch typists.

Speech-activated computers now allow a user to dictate between 30 and 70 words a minute. The speed depends on the specification of the computer and on how long the person has used it to adapt the program to his or her speech pattern.

The conclusion, therefore, is that 95% of computer users could benefit from going over to speech activation.

The Legal Factor

One of the areas of the market that has been picking up well since early 1994 is the use of speech-activated computers in the legal profession.

The legal industry went through a major recession between 1992 and 1994. The legal profession, like the accountancy profession, does not usually suffer during recessional times. Whether other companies go up or go down, they still seem to charge and collect their fees. This time it was different.

Most fee earners in solicitors' practices have two and sometimes three secretaries working for them. This ratio of 1:3 is well known in the industry. Probably for the first time in the past 10 years, the overhead cost of maintaining three secretaries came home to the profession. At the Legal and Solicitors Exhibition at the Barbican I talked to many scores of solicitors about this point, and some partners were boasting when they said that they had reduced the ratio in their practices to 1:2.5.

Fee earners generally dictate their letters and documents into a Dictaphone machine and the tapes are given to the secretary to sort out the documentation. The contract, say, is typed. It goes back to the originator for checking, then back to the secretary for final typing. Finally, the finished document is presented to the fee earner for signature. This procedure usually takes 24 hours, and sometimes 48 hours, a time lag which, in the age of fax communication, is unacceptable.

Fee earners often find themselves working late, needing to get documents out, but not being able to do so because all of the secretarial staff have gone home at the dot of half past five.

Enter speech activation to save the day!

The interesting thing about the legal part of the market is that the majority of fee earners have never touched a keyboard. Because they have always been surrounded by secretarial staff, they have never had to learn to use a word processor, or even touch a computer.

As far as marketing computers is concerned, it is a "double whammy". Not only do fee earners need speech activation, they also need the new and latest technology Pentium computers to run the job on.

However, it all makes financial sense. The cost of a Pentium SpeechWriter is, say, £2999. The cost of a secretary over three years is say £50 000. I rest my case.

The Pentium Factor

We have got to admit that in 1993 the speech-activation products available were not up to the standard that we are seeing today. At that time we had 386 computers on the desk, and had just started seeing the new 486 25 MHz computers arriving.

- *Note:* 25 MHz stands for 25 megahertz. Mega means very big, unusually large, and when talking units means a million. Hertz is a unit of frequency – cycles per second – and was named after the German physicist Heinrich Hertz (1857–1894). A 25 MHz computer is one that has a CPU (central processing unit) chip inside operating at 25 million computational cycles per second.

All of the speech products ran under DOS and they worked passably well, but not so you would give your arm and leg for one. As we moved into 1994 we saw the arrival of the faster 486 computers (66 MHz) and the launch of the Pentium.

- *Note:* A very large number of computers today have their main CPU chip manufactured by Intel. The "Intel Inside" sticker on your computer indicates that the CPU is an Intel one. Intel have captured between 70% and 80% of the CPU market. They are responsible for families of CPUs named 286, 386 and 486. They licensed some other manufacturers to make Intel-designed CPUs and then found that these other companies had started to manufacture their own brands. Because the name was a number, which could not be trademarked, Intel could not legally have any control over this pirating of their technology. Intel, therefore, named their new 586 chip the Pentium processor, so that they could retain control over their new development.

The arrival of the faster 486 computers (66 MHz and now 100 MHz) and now the Pentium has revolutionized the voice-activation market. Intel have already launched their 90 MHz, 100 MHz and 120 MHz Pentium CPUs, and are talking about speeds up to 150 MHz.

Voice activation really comes into its own when there is enough power in the PC to do the necessary computations. In later chapters we will explain why the computer has to have so much power to be voice activated. In general, it can be said that as we move towards a new age of multimedia PCs – one such medium being speech activation – then most business purchasers must look to replacing all of their machines by Pentiums or by the Pentium's successor.

The RSI Factor

Repetitive strain injury or RSI is injury to the fingers, arms and/or shoulders caused by working at the keyboard for too long and too repetitively.

There was a court case in the UK in early 1994, where the judge declared that there was no such illness. However, in the past two years I have had personal contact with scores of people suffering from RSI and it cannot possibly be said that it either does not exist, or is not a major health problem associated with using a PC. I have a friend who cannot even hold an ordinary pen without searing pains going up her fingers and forearm. A mountaineering friend of mine, who was a software programmer, had to give up climbing because of RSI, and even had operations to try to sort out his painful elbows.

Since that legal decision in the UK there have now been many more cases brought and won in favour of RSI sufferers. In general, most large companies are settling out of court in these actions.

In America the situation on this factor is even more interesting. Where people suffer a definable depreciation of their body function because of RSI they can sue their employer for negligence in the workplace. If the employer cannot afford a costly court case and, even if won, there would be no money forthcoming, the lawyers in America are then taking a case against the computer manufacturers as being the culprits in this matter.

The largest manufacturer of PCs in America, Compaq, are now putting warning notices on their keyboards to counteract these claims. Microsoft, who are just bringing out a new ergonomically designed keyboard, are also putting warning notices on their keyboards.

Directors, executives and managers of large corporations (in fact all businesses) will have to bear the RSI factor in mind when they are evaluating whether to speech activate their company's computers. Failure to do so may result in huge compensation claims over the next 10 years. Speech activation may be the only salvation that will rescue them from this financial time bomb.

The Efficiency Factor

There has been an enormous rise in the number of engineering and architectural businesses that are using CAD (computer aided design) terminals to originate drawings. Pentium PCs have the power to deal easily with complex drawing programs such as AutoCad. AutoCad is the most widely used drawing package in the world, and is the program that has set the standard for all other CAD packages that have come onto the market.

In AutoCad you work with a mouse to locate where you want, say, a circle, then you either type in the circle command or move the mouse to the side and click on the circle icon. You then have to type in the centre coordinates and the radius. This moving of the mouse pointer from your point of focus to get items you require is most inefficient. One solution that the industry has come up with is to supply a digitizing palette, with the icon items around the side, which can be operated on a touch basis. The coordinates still have to be typed in.

The use of speech to do all the fetching *and* to enter coordinates solves this inefficiency. Shakespeare's niche product CADSpeak for Windows enables operators to keep the mouse pointer and their attention on the focus of the drawing, and to simply speak in the item required and the co-ordinates of that item. The attention therefore stays at the point of focus. Users have reported an increase of efficiency of up to 25% in using speech activation.

Most drawings also need text labels, which have to be annotated onto the drawing. Speech activation comes into its own when it comes to producing text, and that just makes the draughtsman's task easier.

Another major area where graphic design is used is in the advertising industry. Marketing companies – whether they are using Quark Express, Ventura or PageMaker – have a similar efficiency problem to the draughtsmen of the drawing office. OfficeSpeak Professional also fits the bill here, allowing the graphic designer to produce work more quickly.

In a later chapter we will be discussing how you can utter a speech command (called a speech macro) which will carry out many commands automatically. In complex packages like AutoCad and Quark Express, this one factor can increase the ease of use of the package considerably.

Practice partners and marketing company directors will need to evaluate this increase in productivity as a result of speech activation when planning the introduction of design computers into their offices.

The Hands-Free Factor

If you are an anaesthetist you will need to be working on your patient with your hands, and at the same time recording information into the patient's log – a very good case for a SpeechWriter. There are many other medical situations that would likewise be suitable for operating with a speech-activated computer.

In industry there are many situations on production lines where operators are working with their hands, and their hands are soiled from the job being performed. Operators need to work a keyboard either to record some information or to move the production line on. Special membrane-covered keyboards have been developed to cater for these situations, but in future these can easily be replaced by speech-activated computers.

The On-the-Move Factor

There have been great developments lately by the computer industry to produce sub-notebooks that are no bigger than the size of a small, thin book. These new sub-notebooks are easy to carry around and can be speech activated.

Property surveyors have to walk around buildings making notes of what they find. They normally dictate their reports onto tape, either as they move around the building or later in the car. The tape then goes to the secretary in the office, who types up the report. This has to be checked by the surveyor, and then sent back for final corrections. The whole document cycle can take days, as surveyors are out on site for so much of the time.

Using a sub-notebook SpeechWriter, surveyors can talk in their reports as they do their surveys, then finish them off and even print them out in the car using a small BubbleJet printer. The surveyor can then return to the client, present the "instant" report *and* get paid. You really cannot get more efficient than that.

A clerk taking notes of stock in a large store needs to keep his or her hands free to count the items. The results can be spoken into a small sub-notebook, which is worn around the waist. The sub-notebook can be connected via a wireless network card to the store's computer system. Thus, stock reporting and stock ordering can be done instantly in real time.

Conclusion

This introduction has attempted to explain why there is an unprecedented interest at this time in speech-activated computers.

By giving various examples of how companies are using speech technology, I hope that I have stimulated you into wanting to find out all the facts on this new subject.

The remaining chapters expand on what you can expect now from Speech-Writers, what you can expect in the future, and what you need to know to make buying decisions on computer equipment for your company.

It was predicted by a computer industry survey done in 1994 that by the year 2000 over 85% of all PCs manufactured would be voice activated. There is really no getting away from the fact that you are going to have to get your wits around this subject soon anyway.

Introduction: Series Editor's Notes

Speech-driven computing is changing the way we write, and it will also change the nature of the finished product, the text. It is interesting to note the change in writing style that appears to result from dictating the book to the computer.

When we speak we do not tend to think in terms of using certain detailed forms of punctuation, such as commas or semicolons. Our sentences are less convoluted, our paragraphs shorter. We are less likely to use extended examples, quotations and references. With systems such as SpeechWriter, "what you say is what you get".

The additional concentration required to make intelligent use of the SpeechWriter system may also serve to produce more concise text. There is a process of distillation going on. On revisiting the skeletal framework that results, editing the visual representation of the spoken word, it should be possible to add further details and examples. Having made whisky, it is permissible to add soda, and dilute to taste.

Writing down our words and sentences can make us more self-conscious. We may then add elements of style and presentation, check for repetition, and adjust our vocabulary and expression through processes of editing.

For some people, speech-driven computing will provide a valuable discipline because it requires them to take a fresh approach to a familiar subject. For others, it enables them to bypass the computer keyboard, which may have been a physical or psychological obstacle.

McPherson has written about the technology by using it as a means of communication, building up a powerful and consistent picture which demonstrates the as yet untapped power and potential. It needs to be possible for more people to gain insights into what is going on.

The challenge is to derive practical benefits and to initiate sustainable change. This must involve more people using the technology, but using it for a purpose. This in turn means going beyond simple demonstrations and prepared examples, to practical action.

Speech-driven computing enables speech to be an action. It is not just what you say, but what happens as a result, that is important.

The Future Office

2

A Day at the Office in the Future

You arrive at your company and enter your office. On your desk is the surface mail (often known to those computer buffs who normally use email for all of their correspondence as *snail mail*), which has been opened by your PA. It is very unusual to get surface mail nowadays, because most communication is done by email or on the Internet. Today you receive an actual envelope from the Reader's Digest, who still seem to use this old-fashioned, conservative method of promotion.

On the desk there is a photograph of your spouse, but besides that the office desk is conspicuously empty. It was different a few years ago, when you used to have desktop computers and a lumbering great VDU monitor on the desk.

You put on your MicPhone, which clips behind your right ear and has a small tube that just curves round to the side of your mouth. You reach for your 3D mouse. Both of these devices are cordless.

You say, "Wake up". The large five foot square screen on the wall by your desk lights up and displays your Organizer (Fig. 2.1). The Organizer lists all your appointments for the day, the top priority "to do" list and a pop-up screen showing forthcoming events, which have "reminders" attached to them. You note that it is your spouse's birthday tomorrow and click the mouse to remove the reminders list.

You note that your first appointment today is at 11.30 a.m., so you have 2½ hours to get some real work done. Your top "to do" list item is to ring George Findlay of CityBank to discuss the lease deal regarding Henley Instruments' network installation. You click the Henley Instruments line and say, "More information".

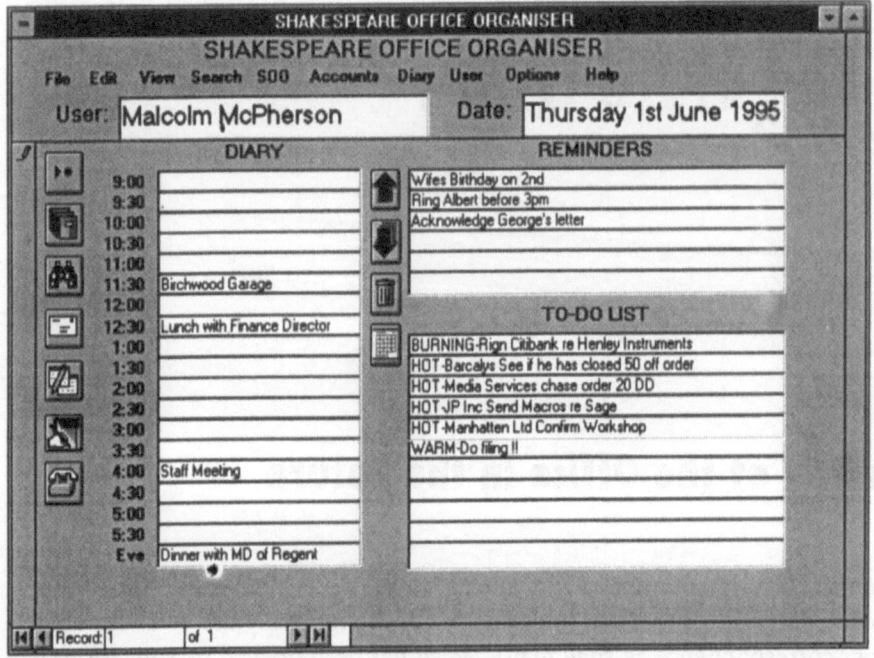

Figure 2.1

A new window overlays the Organizer and lists the details of the client, Henley Instruments (Fig. 2.2). Besides displaying all of the usual details on the company, the window lists the last 10 items of correspondence and notes on the prospect. You click with your mouse on the document line marked as quotation, and say, "Open document". The quotation appears on the screen, so you can go back through it to refresh your mind about the contents.

You say, "Minimize window" to minimize the quotation and notice that there is a "telephone note" that is more recent than the quotation. You click that line and say, "Open document". It is a short note from the sales director, saying that the MD of Henley Instruments has given the go-ahead to install the network subject to finding a good lease purchase rate over three years. You say, "Exit window" to remove the telephone note. You repeat that command to remove the prospect details.

Now you click the telephone icon on the CityBank line of your "to do" list. The Organizer automatically dials the CityBank number, and re-routes your voice to the telephone system. You click the minimized quotation document so that you have the quotation to view while you are talking with George Findlay. On the top right of your screen, George Findlay appears in a small square box. He can see you, because both parties are using video conferencing.

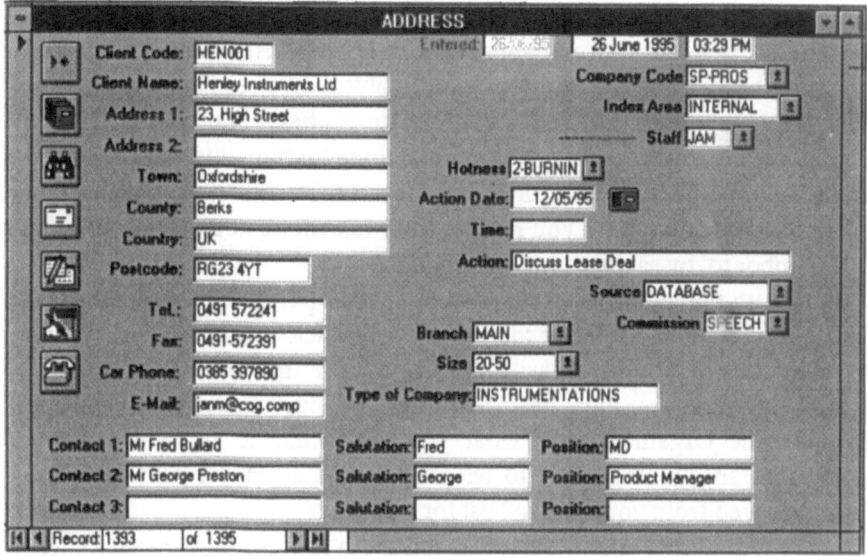

Figure 2.2

The telephone notepad is an area on the screen where you can make notes as the conversation progresses. You click an icon so that you can talk to both the computer and George Findlay at the same time.

"The network system with total price of £12 456.78 would have repayments of £365.67 per month over three years."

You repeat what George has just told you, to confirm the amount he is discussing. At the same time, what you say comes up on the screen.

You finish your conversation, and, when you have disconnected the line by clicking "Disconnect icon", the telephone line is dropped and the voice control reverts to the computer.

You add some clarification to your telephone note, with details of what information the bank requires from Henley Instruments, all done by talking to the computer. You then highlight the information that has appeared in the telephone note, using the mouse. You say, "Copy selection" to put this information into the clipboard (a place where text or a graphic image is stored temporarily). You then close the telephone note by saying, "Close window". The new telephone note will be saved automatically. Because it concerned a supplier, the Organizer asks you if you want to assign the time you spent working with CityBank to a client. It suggests Henley Instruments, because that is the client that you have been working on. You say, "Yes, please", and the time you spent with CityBank is recorded against Henley Instruments. The "to do" list reappears.

You now want to confirm with Henley Instruments the lease figures you have discussed with CityBank. You click on Henley Instruments and say, "New fax". A new letter format appears, with Henley Instruments' name and address at the top, and the fax number and salutation already in place.

The Organizer takes the hassle out of document handling. You never have to worry about naming a file because this is done for you automatically. You only have to concentrate on dictating your fax. In this case you want to confirm the lease details, so you retrieve your telephone note, which you put on the clipboard, by saying, "Paste selection".

You tidy up the letter by dictating some further paragraphs and then say, "Fax document". This will fax the letter automatically to the client. When you return to the "to do" list with "Close window" the letter is saved, and the total time that you have been working on Henley Instruments' case is recorded. The Organizer asks what you now want to do with Henley Instruments, and you schedule to telephone them again the next day. The item is removed from your "to do" list for today.

The telephone rings, and the information that you have on the caller automatically comes up on the screen. A dialogue box asks you if you want to "Take the call", "Refer it to your voice mail" or "Refer it to your PA". It is a supplier, so you say "Refer to voice mail"; you can pick up the message later.

You carry on handling another six items on your "to do" list, then the Organizer reminds you that your visitor, who has an appointment at 11.30, will be here in 10 minutes. You use this time to review the file quickly, ready for the appointment. When the visitor arrives you click the appointment icon so that the time you spend with the client is automatically recorded into the client file.

The above description describes the office of the future – or does it? We have many of these technologies right now. It may come as a surprise to some readers of this chapter that almost all of the items mentioned above can be purchased today.

A list and explanations of them are given in the following subsections.

EMAIL

Email is like a fax facility without paper. You write a letter to someone and send it electronically to their electronic letter box. The recipient reviews the email box every day and picks up your letter, which can be read either in electronic form on the screen or as hard copy by printing it out.

Large companies are using the email system extensively as a normal part of their network services. Lotus and Microsoft have launched email packages, and there are also many other packages available from different software houses.

When a company has a number of branches, and these are joined by an ISDN line, then the email system can work without having to dial the receiving branch.

When you are contacting other companies outside your own, then you have to link into a computer system that is more universal and which gives email facilities. For example, the Grand Met corporation have a service called Metropol, which operates throughout the world. You use your modem to send your email document to a box in their system, and the receiving party picks it up using their own modem. GEC have a similar service. There is also a more academic system known as "the Internet" and another service called Compuserve. All of these give various services for the computer user, including email facilities. Further details are available in the *Executive Guide to Business Electronic Communications.*

This method of sending documents to other companies is very cost effective because normally these services allow you to use a local call to send mail, rather than a long distance or overseas call.

FLAT WALL SCREENS

There have been tremendous advances in the technology of flat screen manufacture. This resulted first in the production of LCD screens for notebooks then, more recently, the manufacture of TFT screens for coloured notebooks.

Both of these technologies allow screens to be built that have a thickness of less than half an inch. These screens so far have been about 9 in × 9 in maximum.

The process of producing a much larger matrix screen or combining a number of the smaller screens into a much larger wall screen has not been perfected. I know of two companies that are working on this project, and there seems to be little doubt that it is possible now, if you are willing to pay a high price for the manufacture.

The process of manufacturing TFT screens is quite arduous, which is why the price has remained fairly high by computer standards. I feel sure that the demand for these high quality coloured screens, both for computers and for digital TVs, will result in a breakthrough very soon.

THE MICPHONE

Receptionists and telephonists have already been subjected to the MicPhone, even if this new nomenclature has never been used for it. Usually, the apparatus looks like a pair of headphones with a small tube bending round to the mouth. It allows the telephonist to hear and to speak to the caller.

The MicPhone is the same, but it only operates into one ear and is very unobtrusive to wear. The future MicPhone will also be cordless, using either wireless waves or infrared waves to communicate with the computer.

Also, it will need to have four channels available, which will cater for all of the modes needed to operate a SpeechWriter as well as to converse with a caller:

1. Speak to the caller only.
2. Speak to the computer only.
3. Speak to both computer and caller at the same time.
4. Speak, but neither the computer nor the caller hears.

THE 3D MOUSE

This beast is already with us!

ALP not only manufacture all Microsoft mice, they have also designed and manufacture a 3D mouse. The mouse looks like a very small shorn-off shotgun. The mouse buttons are where the trigger would normally be. The front disk has three holes in it, out of which come three beams, which are picked up by a plate that is set up in front of the screen. You can use the mouse for operating 3D graphic packages and virtual reality packages.

THE ORGANIZER

There are various Organizers on the market. Lotus have produced one, and another eight from various software houses were reviewed recently in a computer magazine.

The Organizer described in the text above has been produced by Shakespeare and is marketed as Shakespeare Office Organiser. It handles not only diary and "to do" lists but is also a fully-fledged document handler. It has been built as an application with speech activation in mind.

All future application software will need to be developed with a very considered emphasis on operation by speech control.

TELEPHONE DIALLING

Automatic telephone dialling from the screen has been available for several years, but not many users have implemented it. The probable reason is that without a four-mode MicPhone the process becomes somewhat awkward.

Also, automatic dialling needs a modem attached, and it is only over the past year or so that many more computer users have attached modems to their systems. The reason for this has been the increase of users who want to:

- create automatic faxes from their PCs, and/or
- use email facilities from their PCs, and/or
- dial up bulletin boards for information and programs.

Over the next three years modem circuitry, speech card circuitry and network circuitry may very well be built in to the motherboards on all PCs. This would mean that all of these services would be available automatically to the user.

TELEPHONE TRACKING

British Telecom developed a digital method of handling the routing of telephone calls, which is termed System X. In the early days, all calls were handled acoustically using the audio wave form. System X was a way to convert the audio wave form into digital code (a system of 1s and 0s).

Once in this digital form, telephone conversations could be routed much more quickly and much more easily. For a start, British Telecom devised a way of routing several conversation down the wire at the same time. This obviously reduced the number of telephone wires that they needed to erect and maintain.

British Telecom then spent decades upgrading all of their telephone exchanges from the old system to the new one. This has given the UK a much improved system.

British Telecom recently announced an extension to this digitization, in that they now send, at the beginning of each call, a code telling the receiver of the call the number of the calling person. This service is called system Y.

In Shakespeare Office Organiser this code is captured. The company's index of telephone numbers is then searched and the full details of the client, supplier or prospect, if available, are popped up on the screen.

SPEECH-ACTIVATION PACKAGE

The software described in the text above can be driven by commercial packages that are currently available on the market. In the following chapters I describe these packages and outline their specifications, their strengths and their weaknesses.

The Future Office: Series Editor's Notes

McPherson does not require us to imagine a radically different future. Indeed, as he notes, most of the technology concerned is available today.

The chapter started by assuming the continuation of offices as we know them today, rather than suggesting that everyone might work at home. We have come to be sceptical about predictions of wholesale shifts to teleworking and telecommuting, yet at the same time we find that the necessary technology is increasingly available. Our homes and offices are being linked to cable; mobile phones are commonplace; and ambitious executives are installing fax machines at home. The virtual office has no walls, and recognizes no frontiers.

Some readers may be managers with PAs, male and married, and with enthusiasm for five foot square wall screens. Others will be women working from home, at least for a portion of their careers. We can consider the female senior manager working from home, soon after the birth of a baby, giving instructions while her hands are full.

Whether in the office or at home, it is no longer fanciful to talk of speech technology as routinely available.

This need not mean individual purchases. The speech-driven facilities should be available in community telecottages or local business centres, opening up new technology and business decision making to a much wider group of potential managers.

In George Orwell's novel *1984* there were wall screens showing television pictures of Big Brother. Many homes today have numerous large colour television screens, used for one-way broadcasting communication to passive viewers and consumers. The individual could be active as well as simply passive in the use of the new technology.

McPherson's vision is of technology amplifying the effectiveness of the individual, enabling, for example, a woman to be both a mother and a manager, and a disabled individual to perform as effectively as an able-bodied colleague. The technology can be a great leveller, freeing people to compete in the areas that matter.

The convergence of computing and communications technologies means that formerly exotic technologies of electronic mail and video conferencing are becoming more affordable, and real-time moving images are coming to PC screens. Voice control may be necessary to keep the multiplicity of options and media under control.

An emphasis on speech activation will affect the development of application software. Speech activation obliges us to reassess the whole relationship with the computer; it is not simply a matter of changing the interface. Software developers have an urgent need for familiarity with speech technology.

Major industry players are involved: we should expect major initiatives from Intel, IBM and Microsoft, for example. There will be attempts by commercial vendors to seek dominance over the market by imposing their own speech-driven standards.

At this stage in the product development cycle, who are the people with the expertise and experience necessary to reconcile the strengths and weaknesses of the different technologies, combining hardware, software, logic, language and social engineering?

The irony may be that it is small companies like Shakespeare SpeechWriter, uncomplicated by long investments in advanced research, who can see the practical opportunity and push it through to the market, making use of the by-products of research made available through Dragon and other specialist vendors.

Success depends on business users – and other purchasers – seeing the advantage to be gained, and becoming involved. This presents a challenge to service providers in education and training, who need experience in the use of such technologies if they are to be effective in course delivery.

It is not just a question of whether the technology works. It is, however, important to understand the problem, and the different technological solutions now on offer. Without knowledge, executives cannot take informed decisions. The answer is not simply to speak more slowly and loudly.

How Speech Activation Works

3

Simplistic Explanation

The purpose of this book is to give executives an insight into speech activation, what they can expect from it and whether they need to involve their organization or company in this new technology.

However, before we can discuss the finer points of speech activation, before we can look at what packages are on the market, we must first of all explain how it works and introduce the nomenclature and buzz words that executives must understand to be able to get their wits around this subject.

To speech activate a desktop PC, you need to purchase a kit that consists of a headset microphone (Fig. 3.1), a speech card (or Sound Blaster card) and the speech-activation software.

The following description of how it works is a simplistic version to get you going. We will develop our understanding and the finer points of this subject in later chapters.

The microphone is used to "talk in" your words or phases to the computer. If you utter a phrase into the microphone, it goes down the wire as an audio signal to the speech card, which is inside your computer. The speech card then converts the audio signal into a digital representation. What this means is that instead of having a sinusoidal wave pattern, the signal has been converted into a pattern of "offs" and "ons" that looks like this:

11000111001001110010001000011100011

In most of the commercial voice-activation systems each phrase is separated from the others by a silence:

_____   _____   _____

PHRASE 1   PHRASE 2   PHRASE 3

The speech software waits for the silence of, say, a tenth of a second to occur, then gathers up the digital representation of the phrase just uttered. It then does a search of the user's speech pattern, which has been loaded into the computer's memory (Table 3.1).

Table 3.1

Phrase	Digital speech code	Statistic
thank you for	11001111000111100001111100011100	236
thank you for your letter	11001111000011101110111000111	156
think of a good reason	10111111100011100101001010101000	26

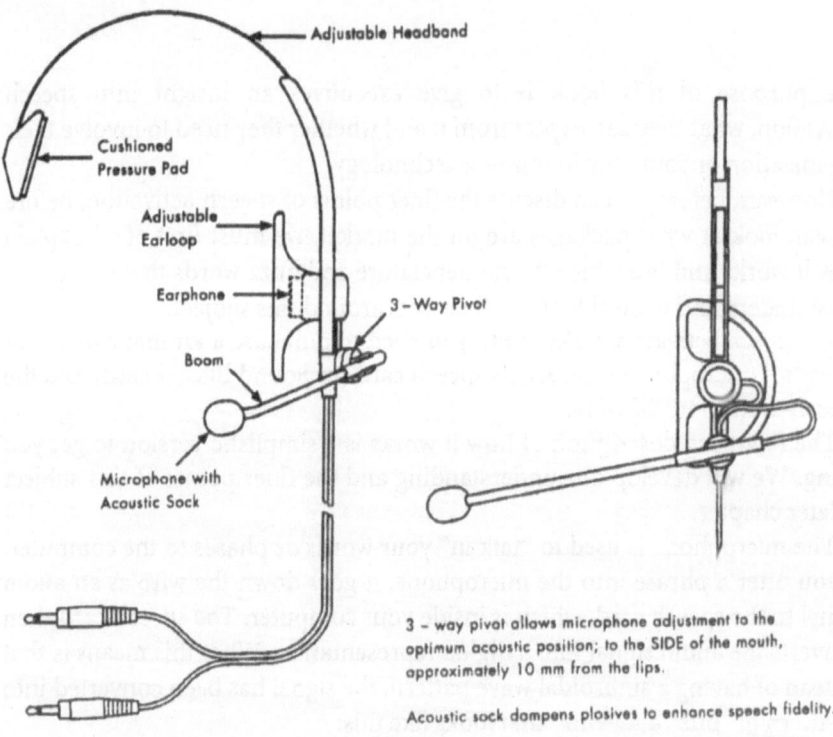

- Adjustable Headband
- Cushioned Pressure Pad
- Adjustable Earloop
- Earphone
- Boom
- Microphone with Acoustic Sock
- 3 – Way Pivot

3 - way pivot allows microphone adjustment to the optimum acoustic position; to the SIDE of the mouth, approximately 10 mm from the lips.

Acoustic sock dampens plosives to enhance speech fidelity.

Figure 3.1

The example in Table 3.1 (opposite) is only three phrases, but a user's speech pattern may contain 1000, 5000, 30000 or even 60000 words or phrases. The speech program searches the digital speech representation code for a match on what has been uttered. If more than one match is obtained, then the program looks at the statistical usage of the phrases, and chooses the phrase that has the highest usage. This phrase is then inserted into the word processor or other application, as though it had been typed using the keyboard. It then waits for the next silence to occur, and the process is repeated.

Continuous Versus Discontinuous

The simplistic explanation above describes a "discontinuous" system of speech activation. Words or phrases have to be said in distinct packages, separated by pauses, for the speech program to understand when to do the recognition process. This represents 90% of the speech products selling in the commercial market at present, but it does not mean that continuous speech may not come into prominence in the next five years, as further research creates better speech-recognition algorithms.

Continuous speech would enable the user to speak in a normal dictation mode on a continuous basis, with no gaps between words or phrases, except where those gaps would naturally occur in normal speech.

The whole method of recognition in continuous speech has to be on a completely different basis. As the program does not know when words and phrases begin and end, it has to analyse each distinct sound or syllable that arrives at the speech card.

For example, if you said, "The cat sat on the mat" the number of distinct sounds (called "phonemes") uttered is 15. The phoneme stream arriving at the speech card has to be digitized, then analysed by the speech program to:

- build the phonemes into words,
- perform sentence analysis on those words to ensure that they make sense, and
- alter them accordingly.

A speech contest is organized annually by the US Defense Advanced Research Projects Agency (DARPA), which is keen to emphasis that it is not a contest to prove who is best, but is to help researchers to learn from each other. A CD was made of 20 people reading passages selected from American business newspapers and magazines. Copies of this CD were sent to all participating universities. The challenge was to devise a speech-recognition system that could read the audio tape, produce the text, and then print it out.

In 1994 the competition was won by the engineering department at Cambridge University, who produced text from the CD with 93% recognition success. Needless to say, the team that devised the computer program used a very high spec RISC (reduced instruction set computer) workstation, and it took several hours for the program to perform the translation. The actual statistic is that the computing time is one hundred times the real time of reading the text.

Many executives ask, "why can't I just dictate into my Dictaphone and then get the computer to translate the tape into a document?". The answer is, of course, you can, as the above competition has shown. However, a 93% efficiency in translation means that in a two-page document of one thousand words you would, using a desktop PC, have to wait six hours for the document to appear and would then have to make sixty corrections.

Obviously, this is not acceptable, but with the advent of very fast computers the situation may change on this methodology very quickly over the next few years.

Speaker-Dependent Versus Speaker-Independent

In a speaker-independent system any person could speak the word or phrase into the microphone, and the computer would understand the utterance, whether it was said with a London accent or a Scottish accent.

"Surely an impossible task," you may retort. Surprisingly, on a small vocabulary basis this is attainable. British Telecom have spent many millions on this particular line of research. On a 12-word vocabulary (0–9, *yes* and *no*) it is possible to get the computer to recognize the utterance, as long as all words are said clearly and distinctly, with obvious pauses between them.

This type of system is used in automatic telephone systems and by banks, to give a service to customers independent of cashiers or operators.

This type of small, speaker-independent, speech-activation system could also be used to control machinery where very few instructions are required. There are very few examples of this to date because of the "error factor" inherent in speech activation. In other words, the system is likely to get it wrong sometimes, and that could be catastrophic.

We will be exploring the "inherent error" nature of speech activation in a later chapter. It can be overcome by adapting the application software to take account of this factor.

Most of the speech-activation systems being sold at present are speaker-dependent systems. That is, the user has to train the words and phrases using his or her own voice, before being able to use the program for dictation or command purposes.

If you have a computer that has the speech-activation kit installed, it does not mean that it can only be used by one person, however. Each person builds up his or her own vocabulary words, digital speech codes and statistics, which collectively are known as the "speech pattern".

Each person using the terminal has his or her own speech pattern, which is loaded into the memory from the hard disk of the computer at the beginning of a dictation session. If any changes are made to the speech pattern during the period of use, then the changed speech pattern will have to be re-saved to the hard disk at the end of the session.

In the next section we will be discussing the different vocabulary sizes. On large vocabulary systems (more than 5000 words or phrases), it is usual to set up a "standard" speech pattern, which can be used by each new user and go some way towards relieving the person from the inconvenience of having to train every word or phrase that will be used.

The way in which these standard voice patterns are manufactured is interesting. First of all, if the speech pattern is going to contain 20 000 words, then the manufacturer has to decide which 20 000 words are to be included. Secondly, the normal way of getting a "standard" speech pattern is to have 50 people train the 20 000 words (say each one three times), and then overlay the digital speech codes on top of each other to give an average final pattern.

Because male and female voices tend to be pitched very differently, certain manufacturers have done both as separate sets. You can imagine that creating such standard speech patterns is an extremely costly business, and one that very few manufacturers have embarked upon.

When a new user starts to talk to the computer, the words used are compared with this standard speech pattern. As there are many differences in the way that people speak, and because of regional accents, the hit rate at the beginning is not very good. A hit rate of even 90% equates to about 80 words wrong in a two-page dictation. If the user corrects each wrong word that occurs, and thus alters the standard speech pattern closer to his or her own speech pattern, then the hit rate will gradually improve.

There is another school of thought that believes that, in the long run, with a speaker-dependent system it is better for the user to train his or her own speech pattern from scratch, because this means that it is very close to 100% from square one, and the speech pattern is not cluttered with words that the user will never utter.

Small Vocabulary Versus Large Vocabulary

There are five vocabulary ranges that seem to be filtering out of the speech market as it gathers momentum. Table 3.2 gives a view of these ranges. These vocabulary quantities refer to the number of words, phrases and commands that are possible in the user's own speech pattern.

Table 3.2

Label	Range	Uses	Examples
Tiny	1–128	Tele Systems and controlling machines	Telephone and Bank Services
Small	129–1024	Controlling CAD and graphics packages	CADSpeak for Windows
Medium	1025–8196	Database handling and paragraph generation	Dragon Starter OfficeSpeak Lite
Large	8197–32768	General business dictation	Dragon Classic IBM PDS OfficeSpeak
Very large	32769–65536	Scientific, professional and writer dictation	Dragon Power IBM PDS

For example, in the DragonDictate Classic package the base vocabulary is 30 000, which is a fixed maximum number. The 30 000 vocabulary user's speech pattern database resides in memory, and is searched each time an utterance is made. There are also dictionary files that may contain 120 000 words and voice models, but these are only searched when a correction cycle is being performed.

The speed and accuracy of speech recognition depends in part on the way in which the user's speech pattern database is searched. In a later chapter we will go into the different methods that are used by the different products, and how developments in artificial intelligence (AI) are affecting these methods.

Suffice it to say that the smaller the vocabulary, the higher the likelihood of 100% recognition. To counter this, the smaller the vocabulary, the more likely you are to run out of words!

There are ways around the vocabulary size. For example, in Shakespeare's CADSpeak for Windows product, which is used to operate AutoCad, the speech pattern database addressed at any one time is 900 words and/or commands. However, there is a system of vocabulary switching, which allows up to 40 separate vocabularies with a total word size of 10 000 utterances. All of the vocabularies can be kept in memory to make the system run faster, but only one of them is accessed at any one time.

The user in this case has full control over the content and switching of these vocabularies. When you first load in OfficeSpeak Professional, you are in the AutoCad vocabulary, which is used for ordinary AutoCad commands. When you want to put a label on the drawing you are producing, you say [SWITCH TO LABEL], which gives you access to up to 900 label utterances that will put various labels onto your drawing. When you want to draw some piping on your drawing, you say [SWITCH TO PIPE], and so on.

The companies producing much larger vocabulary products will probably say that vocabulary switching is completely unnecessary, because their products work just as well with just a large block of 30 000 utterances, which is searched all the time.

The point really is the accuracy and the speed of the search. When you are preparing a delicate and complicated drawing, you do not want a misunderstood utterance to suddenly wipe out your work.

There is another point to segmented vocabularies. In the next section we will be developing the difference between a word, a phrase and a command. Each of these can be activated by an utterance. We tend, therefore, to talk of the number of utterances instead of the number of words.

If you have one big block of speech pattern, it is quite difficult to track and do housekeeping on the words, phrases and commands you have in that block. When you have small vocabulary sizes of, say, 100, 500 or even 1000 words, you can view these quite easily and pass these utterances in small groups from one vocabulary to another.

Also, you can pass a diskette to another user and say, "import the AGS.VOC file [the speech pattern file for Andrew Saunders]. It contains all those speech macros I showed you".

If you transfer 100 specialist speech pipe macros, it is a 10 minute task to train the commands in your own voice and be up and operating with them immediately.

We have talked mostly in this chapter about voice-dependent systems. Virtually all of these operate on a statistical database search process. Therefore, voice recognition is prone to error, and users should take that into account in the use to which they put speech activation.

The software written up until now has not taken speech activation into account. It therefore does not make the necessary checks that are needed to make it "speech safe". This is a completely new subject, and one that will probably be given a lot of thought in the next 10 years.

Dalek Speak Versus Phrase Speak

There are three types of utterance:

- A *word*, which is where you say the word "table" and *table* comes up on the screen.
- A *phrase*, which is where you say "Thank you for" and *Thank you for* comes up on the screen.
- A *command*, which is where you say [UNDERLINE TEXT] and the text that you have highlighted is automatically underlined.

You will notice that when we refer to a command we put it in square brackets. This is the convention in speech activation to make commands stand out from ordinary dictation text (words and phrases).

A command has associated with it a series of keystrokes (called a voice macro) that carries out some function in the application package being run. For example, you could say [FAVOURITE SPREADSHEET] and have the computer load in your sales forecast spreadsheet automatically.

Usually, commands are given "double barrel" names so that they do not get confused with ordinary words. When you say the command you must remember to say it all in one go without pausing between the words, otherwise the SpeechWriter will get it confused with the word "favourite" followed by "spreadsheet".

The same rule applies if you want to put in a phrase. If you put in "Thank you for" as a phrase, it must be said as though it is one word.

The diagram at the beginning of this chapter applies very much to the way in which speech systems handle words, phrases and commands. Each must be said as though it is a word, and a gap must be left between utterances:

COMMAND	PHRASE	WORD

During 1993 we were all using speech systems based on words. (Even today the IBM Personal Dictation System and DragonDictate are still based on individual words.) The term "dalek speak" was coined because of the way that you had to communicate with your computer.

The alternative would be a continuous speech system, which would analyse your whole sentence as it flowed and get it right. The feeling in the industry is that it will be at least five years, and probably ten, before a large vocabulary, user-independent, continuous speech system will be available.

Some small vocabulary, continuous speech systems have already been announced, and so such a system will come in time. It depends not only on the ingenuity of the software writer, but also very much on the power of the desktop computer to do the sort of computations required in analysing continuous speech.

In 1994 Shakespeare announced a half-way house. Together with Sussex University, they researched the use of phrases rather than individual words, and launched their "Phrase Technology".

Instead of saying:

"Thank" "you" "for" "your" "letter" "of" "the" "15th" "of" "November"

you say:

"Thank you for" "your letter of" "the 15th of November"

It is more natural to talk in phrases than in individual words. If you examine a person dictating into a Dictaphone, you will find that he or she will dictate in small bursts, and not in a continuous manner.

It is a matter of having the executive use phrases rather than individual words. It is a methodology and has its own discipline.

Executives using this technology have reported that it gives a much better recognition rate, as well as being a more comfortable way of talking to the computer. The explanation for this higher recognition rate is that if you say, for example, the word "is" the SpeechWriter has only one small sound on which to do its search of the database. It will invariably get it confused with "his" and "this". On the other hand, "this is a" said as a phrase consists of several sounds, which means that the search is far more positive because the system has more to go on.

Conclusion

In this chapter we have attempted to give you some insight into how speech activation works and some of the issues that are operative when the executive talks into the computer.

In the next chapter we will review some products and walk you through using them. In this way we want you to get a feel for how you would actually use a SpeechWriter if you had one.

How Speech Activation Works: Series Editor's Notes

Speech activation does not depend on magic, but on processing patterns of information. It may soon become routine. Understanding is increasing regarding continuous and discontinuous speech systems, speaker-dependent and speaker-independent systems, and the trade-off between large vocabulary and reliability.

There are valuable lessons to be learned from Japan, which was poorly served by computer keyboards, considering the scale of the written and printed character set. Speech provided an opportunity to bypass an unnecessary obstacle, and companies have prospered by identifying attainable goals and deliverable projects. Companies have been motivated to take part, because their survival may depend on effective use of speech technology. There has not been similar pressure in the UK to date.

One Japanese tendency is to find a pragmatic and attainable compromise between the present situation and the ideal. The present state of the art of technology will not support continuous speech, so less satisfactory alternatives must be explored.

McPherson introduces both "dalek speak" and "phrase speak". As the idea of "dalek speak" and "phrase speak" is introduced, we may find we are reminded of the simple principles of programming. We are accustomed to using natural language in verbal communication, and to being obliged to use a computer language when using a computer. For "phrase speak" to be successful, as McPherson says, there needs to be method and discipline.

"Phrase speak" is not necessarily a half-way house to continuous speech. Rather, it is a way of packaging cliches and standard utterances for the group, culture or "form of life" concerned, for reasons of ease and efficiency. Considerable time will be saved if several users share a common vocabulary, with which they associate their respective speech patterns.

Users of a phrase-speak system will be constrained to locally approved idiom, if efficiency is to be maintained. On the positive side, it should be possible to identify target markets where this cultural constraint is appropriate: bureaucracies, multinational organizations and total institutions (armed forces, prisons, hospitals, school administrations etc.). One could imagine "power users" or local language and IT consultants offering appropriate vocabularies.

We will hear claims that, with the advent of speech technology, the need for programming is past. This cannot be true. Programming will simply take a different form.

It has taken several decades for us to realize how little we know about computing using formal languages. Computers can only deal with binary information, but our use of natural language is much richer and vaguer, with shades and nuances of meaning. We cannot escape from the problems of formalism by using a speech interface. We may instead be adding new layers of complication, and providing the illusion of ease of use of the technology in general.

Example Speech Packages

Introduction

In this chapter I am going to describe two packages in depth, to give you an idea of what purchasing a speech-activation package entails. I will describe how you install it, how you train your speech patterns and then how you operate it in everyday use.

The first package that I am going to describe is *OfficeSpeak Lite*, which has a medium-sized vocabulary capability of 10 000. This capacity almost puts it in the large vocabulary range, but the vocabulary is segmented into up to 40 different vocabularies, each of which can house up to a maximum of 900 words, phrases or commands.

The total vocabulary cannot exceed 10 000 utterances, although it would be theoretically possible to have 36 000 commands. For example, the command [OPEN WORK DOCUMENT] could appear in four different vocabularies with four different macros associated with it but would only count as one utterance, because it is always said in the same way, no matter which package you are operating.

OfficeSpeak Lite is a low entry Windows package that enables the user to navigate all Windows packages, do simple dictation and paragraph generation in Word, handle spreadsheet entry in Excel and handle database applications in Access. It can be adapted to work with any Windows product. The package is a very good, inexpensive introduction to speech activation. It assumes that you have a certified 16-bit multimedia sound card, like the later editions of the Sound Blaster card. It comes with a headset microphone, two 1.44 Mb diskettes and a manual. It needs 8 Mb to run Windows applications and speech comfortably.

The second package is *DragonDictate for Windows* (Classic edition), which has a large-sized vocabulary capacity of 30 000. The vocabulary is divided into small control vocabularies to navigate Windows and specific applications, and a very large dictation vocabulary, which is preset with about 29 000 words. It also has a large 120 000 reference dictionary, containing words and "mean" voice models.

DragonDictate for Windows is an "author orientated" dictation package, which can be used for producing long and varied reports. It is ideal for journalists, writers of books and executives who have to produce long and mixed reports. It can be adapted to work with any Windows product. The package is probably the best Windows large vocabulary dictation product on the market at this time. It comes with an ACPA sound card, a Shure headset microphone and 12 diskettes. It needs at least 16 Mb to run Windows applications and speech comfortably, and often users have to have 20 Mb or 24 Mb to be comfortable.

OFFICESPEAK LITE: INSTALLATION

The manual for this package contains a whole chapter on the installation of the sound card and the software. On the installation diskette there is also a README.WRI file, which gives additional information on different sound cards.

The program itself is contained on one diskette; it is a very compact piece of programming code. There is an additional diskette that contains a sample speech file with vocabulary commands and phrases for Windows programs like File Manager, Microsoft Word 6, Excel, Powerpoint and Access.

The software is installed like any other Windows program by clicking the "Run" option in the "File" menu and entering A:\SETUP{Enter}. The program allows you to install on any subdirectory with a default of C:\SPEECH.

A note here about operating this package on a network: it is essential that it is installed on a hard disk local to the workstation. That can be either C: or D: if there are two hard disks present. Once operational, OfficeSpeak Lite can be used to operate any Windows program on the fileserver or on the local hard disks.

When the files have been copied across, a group folder is automatically set up with a program icon to start the package. The package allows up to five users but each user has a separate speech pattern. The user's speech pattern needs to be loaded into the memory of the computer before that person can speak to the computer. The facility can only be used by one user at a time.

OFFICESPEAK LITE: TRAINING YOUR SPEECH PATTERN

Once the installation procedure has been completed, the OfficeSpeak Lite application will appear as an icon in a new Shakespeare SpeechWriter folder on the Windows desktop. If you want the SpeechWriter to come up each time you enter Windows copy the icon to the "Start-up" folder on your desktop.

To activate the package from the Shakespeare SpeechWriter folder, double-click with the mouse on the icon and OfficeSpeak Lite will load. Alternatively, the cursor keys can be used to highlight the icon and the package activated by pressing the {Enter} key.

Once activated, the pop-up box, shown below, will appear. To proceed you will have to enter your name in the box.

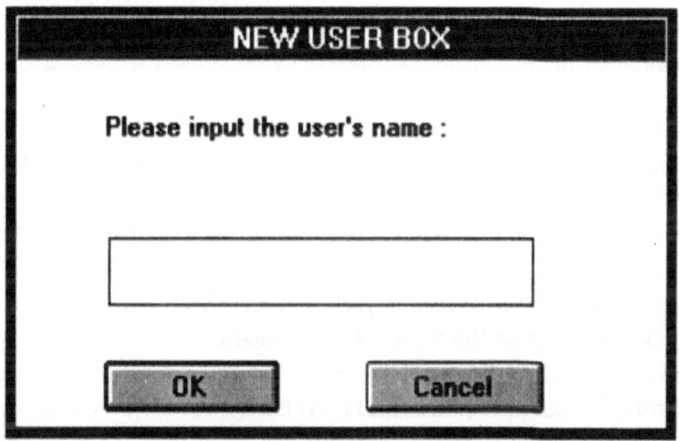

You put your forename and surname name in the name box. If you put "John Brown" a new speech file J-B.VOC is created. The J-B.VOC file contains the words, phrases and commands (with their macros); when you start to train the system a J-B.USR file is set up to house the cross-referenced utterances (i.e. the digital representation of the sounds of these words, phrases and commands).

Before you begin you must check the following:

- Your microphone is correctly attached.
- You are wearing the microphone correctly (i.e. at the side of your mouth, about half an inch away).
- You are comfortable.

You should now click on OK in the name box to start the training. After a few seconds the training pop-up box appears, as follows:

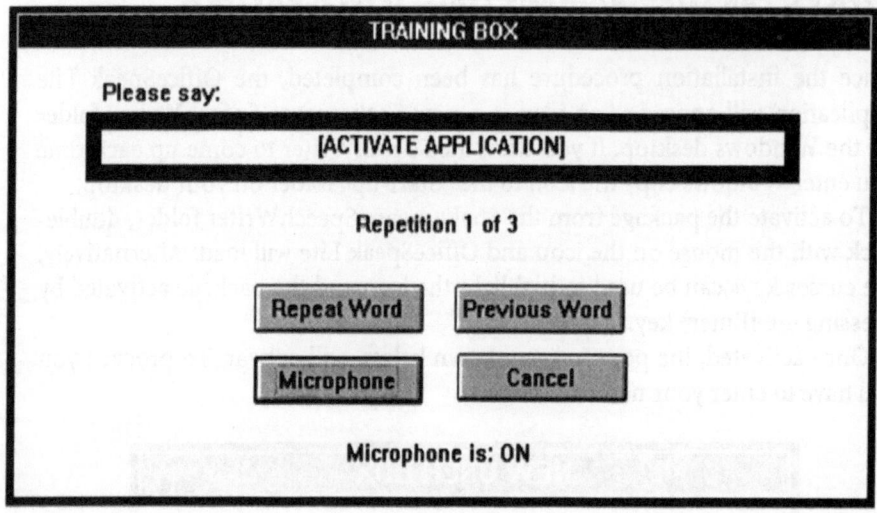

Each word, phrase or command that is to be trained appears in the heavy bordered box in the training window. Square brackets enclose any command that is to be trained in OfficeSpeak Lite.

OfficeSpeak Lite recognizes your speech by recording three repetitions of each word. You say each word three times separated by a small pause. If you stumble over a word the system analyses that the three samples are *not* the same and makes you repeat the three trainings again.

If you have to say more than one word (i.e. when the utterance is a phrase or a command), for example [ACTIVATE FILE MANAGER], then say them as one word *without* a pause between the words.

This initial training consists of thirty words, which takes about four minutes. The commands you train are from two vocabularies.

The *Desktop* vocabulary gives commands that allow you to move around the Windows Program Manager desktop, such as:

[MOVE LEFT]
[MOVE RIGHT]
[ACTIVATE WORD 6]

The *Dictation* vocabulary contains useful commands such as:

[NEW LINE]
[FULL STOP]
[COMMA]

OFFICESPEAK LITE AFTER THE INITIAL TRAINING SESSION

When you have finished the first training session you are ready to start talking to your computer through OfficeSpeak Lite.

You will notice that at the top of the screen, overlaid on the desktop, is the Shakespeare Information Bar.

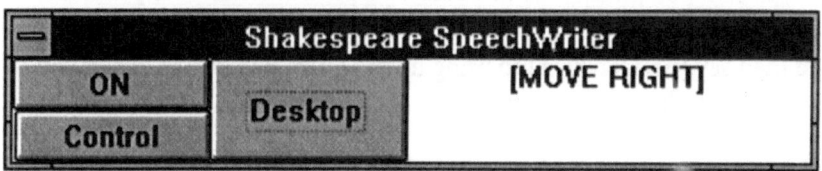

The commands that you have just trained can now be used. If you are in a Windows folder, such as the Microsoft Office folder, then you can move the focus (i.e. the highlighting) around using speech. If you say [MOVE RIGHT] the focus will move one icon to the right.

The information bar tells you the current state of the speech system. The "On" button indicates whether the microphone is on or off, the "Control" button, if clicked, displays the Shakespeare "Control" menu, the "Desktop" button displays the current vocabulary you are accessing and the white window displays the utterance you have just said.

If you move the focus to the Microsoft Word 6 icon and say [ACTIVATE APPLICATION] the Word package will be loaded.

The active vocabulary will still be the Desktop vocabulary. To change it to the Dictation vocabulary you say [SWITCH TO DICTATION]. Note that vocabulary switching can be done automatically. This is discussed later, in the section entitled "Operating with Commands Using OfficeSpeak Lite".

ADDING WORDS OR PHRASES TO OFFICESPEAK LITE

Except for the few commands that you trained at the beginning, you really have a clean slate when it comes to words and phrases in your Dictation vocabulary. You can add up to 40 vocabularies and each vocabulary can contain up to 900 words, phrases or commands.

Phrases can be added as you go along or you can copy large lists of phrases from the speech pattern of another user, who has already set up and works with those vocabularies. You just train these phrases three times, and they can then be used when you are dictating your documents.

To add a word or phrase while you are dictating, you say the phrase. If the active vocabulary does not contain that phrase then the Information Bar will show four question marks to indicate that the utterance has not been understood.

You then say [ENTRY BOX] to bring up the Entry Box, which allows you to enter in new words and commands.

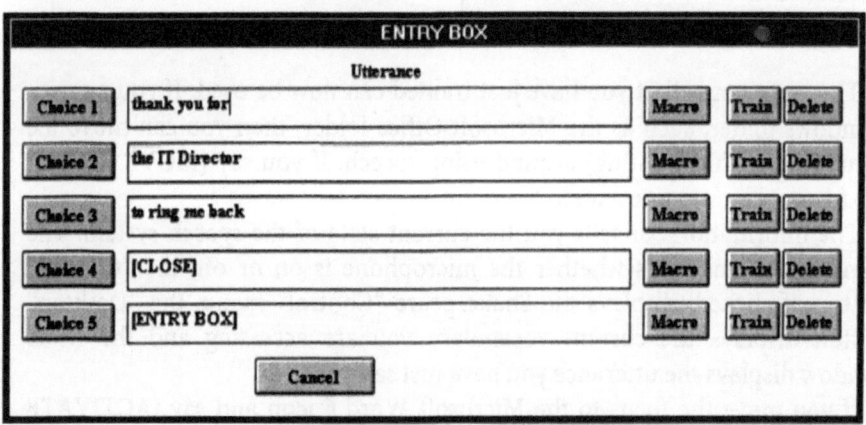

For example, if you were entering the phrase "thank you for", you would type it into the Choice 1 box. You then click the TRAIN button and train the phrase three times, as usual. The Entry Box then disappears and the phrase appears in your word processing document. That phase will never have to be typed again, and will be ready for you to use in the future when you are dictating your documents.

CORRECTING A WORD OR PHRASE USING OFFICESPEAK LITE

If you utter a phrase and the system misunderstands and puts another phrase into the text, this is corrected using the Entry Box. You activate the Entry Box by saying [ENTRY BOX]; it will show the phrase the system thought you said in the Choice 1 box. It will also show other phrases it thought you might have said in the other five choice boxes. If the phrase you want in your text is, say, the one in the Choice 3 box, you can activate it immediately by clicking the CHOICE 3 button. This will also train the phrase once and alter the speech pattern for that word accordingly. If you want to retrain the word from scratch then you can click the TRAIN button opposite Choice 3 and train the phrase three times.

If the phrase is not in the Entry Box but is in the vocabulary, you can start to type it in. You will notice that the system goes through the vocabulary listing and shows you the phrases that it has in alphabetical order; your phrase will appear after you have typed a few characters of it. In this case, because the system got it completely wrong, the system insists you train the word three times whether you press the CHOICE button or the TRAIN button.

You can at any time during dictation revert to the keyboard to enter or correct a phrase or word.

A note here to say that there is a difference in approach with OfficeSpeak Lite, compared to most of the other large dictation packages. For example, with DragonDictate for Windows a new user is given a 30 000 vocabulary, where all the words have a preset "mean" speech pattern. In DragonDictate, when a word is corrected the program has to try to adapt the mean pattern to how you have just pronounced the word. With OfficeSpeak Lite the speech pattern is *exactly* your own, because it is always built from scratch. The difference in recognition ability because of this factor and because of the smaller 900 vocabulary size is very pronounced: OfficeSpeak Lite is between 99% and 100%; DragonDictate for Windows between 85% and 95%.

OPERATING WITH COMMANDS USING OFFICESPEAK LITE

OfficeSpeak Lite and DragonDictate for Windows are both WYSIWYG packages: what you *say* is what you get. This means that when you are dictating a letter the phrases go straight into the word processing package you are using, in real time.

This must be compared with the IBM PDS system (now called IBM Voice-Type: IBM renamed it because they did not like their Personal Dictation System being called by the acronym PDS), which is not WYSIWYG.

In the PDS system you speak into a "Dictation Window" at the bottom of the screen, and this text is later transferred to your word processor. Also, because the IBM system is doing sentence analysis as well as recognition, the words appearing in the Dictation Window run about two to three words behind your speech, so it is confusing to look at the screen anyway until you have to go back over the text and correct the mistakes.

In OfficeSpeak Lite the user operates in real time all of the time, even when performing commands. For example, if you want to go into bold text you say [BOLD FONT], which operates a macro that presses {Ctrl+b}, making all text that follows emboldened. To turn off the bold font you repeat the command.

Note that the bold hotkey {Ctrl+b} is a toggle. If repeating the command is not natural enough, you can define two commands, [BOLD ON] and [BOLD OFF], which both send the {Ctrl+b} key combination.

To enter a command you say [ENTRY BOX]. When the blank Entry Box appears you type in the command as [BOLD FONT]. The convention that is adopted is that commands are contained in square brackets and are always in upper case.

Connected to each command there must be a series of keystrokes, called a macro. If you do not attach a macro to a command and try to exit from the Entry Box you will get an error message to that effect. To enter the macro you press the **MACRO** button to the right of the command name you have just entered. The following dialogue appears:

```
┌──────────────────────────────────────────────────┐
│                       WORD                         │
│                                                    │
│  Utterance :                                       │
│                                                    │
│  [INCREASE FONT SIZE]                              │
│                                                    │
│  Macro :                                           │
│                                                    │
│  {CTRL+>}                                          │
│                                                    │
│                                                    │
│                                                    │
│                                                    │
│                                                    │
│   ┌──────────┐   ┌──────────┐    ◉ Key Mode       │
│   │    OK    │   │  Cancel  │                      │
│   └──────────┘   └──────────┘    ○ Type Mode      │
│                                                    │
└──────────────────────────────────────────────────┘
```

The macro can be typed in as {Ctrl+b} or the "Key Mode" radio button can be pressed and then the macro can be entered by pressing the keys for the correct combination. When the macro has been entered the command can be trained like any ordinary word or phrase.

Once the command has been trained it can be used in real time to move smoothly from regular font into bold font and then back to regular font.

WORKING WITH VOCABULARIES WITH OFFICESPEAK LITE

Having to work out and type every Word 6 command is of course a little like re-inventing the wheel. The vocabulary manager of OfficeSpeak Lite enables the user to copy the full list of Word 6 commands into his or her own speech pattern in a few minutes. In fact, there are 69 Microsoft Word commands supplied on the sample speech pattern diskette; these would take about 10 minutes to train.

To invoke the Vocabulary Manager in OfficeSpeak Lite, the vocabulary name button is clicked or you say [VOCABULARY]. The following dialogue appears:

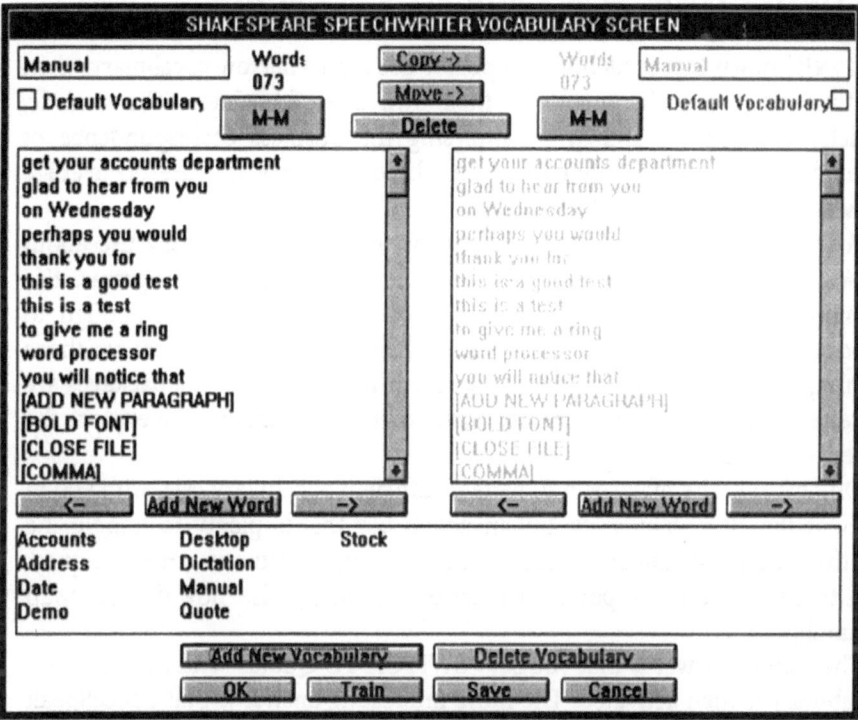

The first step would be to press the ADD NEW VOCABULARY button and set up a Word vocabulary. Then press the right-hand J-B button and when the directory dialogue appears click on the Z-Z.VOC vocabulary. This sample vocabulary appears in the right-hand window, and by clicking at the bottom of the vocabulary list the Word vocabulary is displayed in the right-hand list. You can then see the new empty J-R Word vocabulary on the left and the full Z-Z Word vocabulary on the right. By clicking the COPY button at the top the commands can be copied across.

The commands can be trained in 10 minutes. Not all of the 69 commands will be used in your dictation, so individual commands can be copied across from the Word vocabulary to, say, the Dictation vocabulary when they are required. The commands do not need to be retrained if they are copied to a new directory because the utterance has already been trained. Thus, you can italicize, underline, increase font size, save and print your documents within a quarter of an hour of installing the package.

In a similar way, a list of phrases for a particular vocabulary can be copied from an existing user to a new user. The training time is minimal compared to the time it saves in being able to dictate fluently in some area of a profession.

ADVANCED TECHNIQUES USING OFFICESPEAK LITE

It is well known that most business people use a very narrow vocabulary when writing letters and documents in their own line of business. The statistic, which has been researched by analysing the business correspondence of individual executives, is that during a whole year they will use on average between 4000 and 6000 different words.

Another interesting statistic is that most business people only use about 20% of the facilities of their most frequently used software programs. For example, if executives use Word and Excel, they usually learn enough to produce the documents and spreadsheets they require and then just use those techniques for the next five years. The rest of the facilities of the packages are never even considered, because executives do not have the time to explore the other possibilities.

OfficeSpeak Lite may seem to have insufficient vocabulary size, with 900 in each of the 40 vocabularies, but in actual use this is plenty to handle the relatively small vocabularies used by most executives. However, the one question that is asked by all potential users of the package is, "how do you swap vocabularies?".

The simple answer is that you say "SWITCH TO Quotes" and the "Quotes" vocabulary is then activated. The more interesting answer is that OfficeSpeak Lite has the facility to switch vocabularies "on the fly" without the user having to worry about the switching.

There are advanced macro techniques that allow the user to operate such vocabulary switching techniques quite simply. Let us take the example of putting dates within the text of a document. Entering a date in a document means that you would have to be able to dictate 31 dates such as "the 15th of" and 12 months such as "April", which could also put out the year automatically.

These 43 phrases could be put into each Dictation vocabulary but this is wasteful of vocabulary space when just one vocabulary can be used, as long as there is automatic vocabulary switching. In OfficeSpeak Lite there is a facility to switch vocabularies within a command. In this case, entering a date would be preceded by the phrase "your letter of", for example. Instead of making this a simple phrase, it is made into a command as follows:

[YOUR LETTER OF]

This has a macro associated with it:

your{SPACE}letter{SPACE}of{SPACE}{SWITCHTO+Date}

The final key combination {SWITCHTO+Date} automatically switches the vocabulary to the "Date" vocabulary. In the Date vocabulary you can dictate the day and then the month. When you dictate the month, this again is a command, which has a macro that puts out the month and the year and switches back to whatever earlier vocabulary you were operating in:

[APRIL] April{SPACE}1995{SPACE}{SWITCHBACK}

Thus, the user dictating the text does not have to think about switching vocabularies because it is done automatically. There are other advanced techniques available in OfficeSpeak Lite, but it is best that these are learned when you start to use the package.

CONCLUSION ON OFFICESPEAK LITE

We hope that the above summary gives a good idea about how you would operate the package. The executives whom we have interviewed who have used the package say that it did not take very long to get the hang of talking to their computers, and that this package gave them a good feel for this new innovative technology.

Many of the users of OfficeSpeak Lite have upgraded to OfficeSpeak, which has greater macro power, is not restricted to 40 vocabularies, is hands free and has access to various dictionaries so that each phrase does not have to be typed in. Other users have upgraded to DragonDictate for Windows if they found that they needed a large vocabulary system for more general documents.

There is no doubt that executives who want to experience this new technology can do no wrong in getting this package and playing with it. It will give them an idea of how far the speech activation industry has progressed.

DRAGONDICTATE FOR WINDOWS: INSTALLATION

The manual to this package contains a whole chapter on the installation of the sound card and the software. On the installation diskette there is also a README.WRI file that contains last-minute information about Dragon-

Dictate for Windows.

The program itself is contained on 12 diskettes, which contain the program, the 30 000 mean user's speech pattern and the 120 000 dictionary.

The software is installed like any other Windows program by clicking the "Run" option in the "File" menu and entering A:\SETUP{Enter}. The program allows you to install in any subdirectory with a default of C:\DDWIN.

A note here about operating this package on a network: it is essential that the package is installed on a hard disk local to the workstation. That can be either C: or D: if there are two hard disks present. Once operational, DragonDictate for Windows can be used to operate selective Windows programs on the fileserver or on the local hard disks.

When the files have been copied across, a group folder is automatically set up with several icons associated with the package. Each package that is activated by speech from DragonDictate also has to be in this group folder. When the folder is initially set up you will see the following program icons, which have been copied across automatically:

- DragonDictate (starts the program)
- Vocabulary Manager
- Tutorial
- DragonDictate Help
- DragonDictate Read Me
- Program Manager
- File Manager
- Write
- Cardfile
- Calendar
- Calculator
- Clock
- Notepad

If you want other packages to be activated by voice you will need to copy them into the DragonDictate for Windows folder using the "Copy" command in the "File" menu of the Windows desktop.

The package is able to handle an unlimited number of users (limited only by the space on the hard disk) but each user has a separate speech pattern. The user's speech pattern needs to be loaded into the memory of the computer before that person can speak to the computer. The facility can only be used by one user at a time.

DRAGONDICTATE FOR WINDOWS: TRAINING YOUR SPEECH PATTERN

When DragonDictate has been installed you click the program icon and the package asks you to enter your name:

When the user's speech pattern is set up the program creates a subdirectory based on the first eight letters of the forename plus any required letters from the surname, with no spaces noted. In this example, the subdirectory will be C:\JOHNBROW.

Within this subdirectory there will be a \CURRENT\ subdirectory, which houses the speech pattern of the user. When the speech pattern has been saved a number of times a \BACKUP\ subdirectory is set up to house the backup files.

The installation program asks you for the type of microphone: the standard microphone is the Shure SM10A headset. Most microphones supplied by Dragon resellers are compatible with the Shure specification.

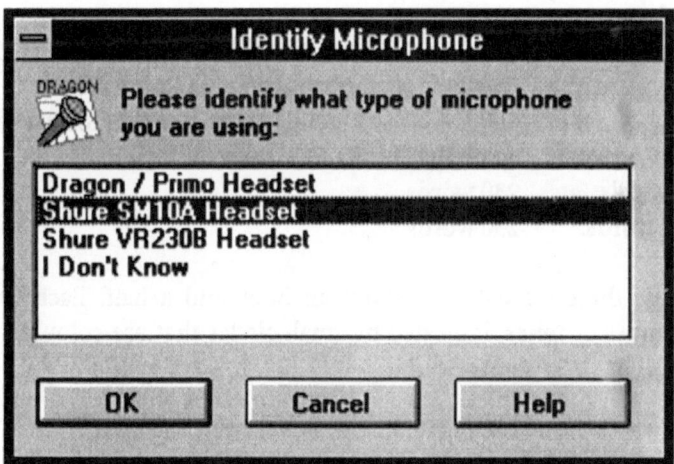

The user's speech pattern is now set up and the program asks you to say about 10 words so that it can ensure that your microphone is working correctly and adjust the speech patterns slightly, depending on how you pronounce these words.

It immediately asks if you wish to do the tutorial, and that is recommended. A cartoon dragon appears on the screen and takes you through the main principles of operating the package.

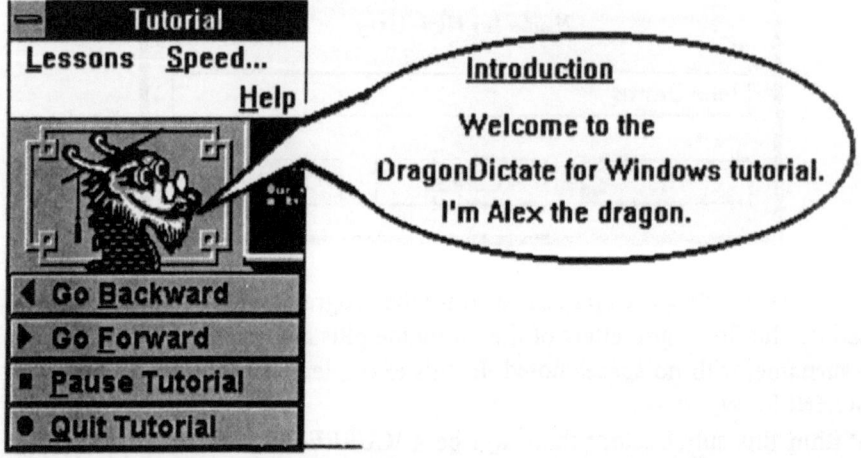

The full tutorial takes nearly an hour if you do all of the sections. During the tutorial the system is learning how you speak to a limited degree.

After the tutorial the program asks you if you would like to run the "Quick Training", because this improves your recognition accuracy when you start using the product. The Quick Training has four sections with a total of 745 words. The four groups are:

correction words:	65 words (including the phonetic alphabet)
common commands:	200 words (including many punctuation words and symbols)
dictation words:	230 words
additional words:	250 words

To train all of these words takes about an hour and a half. Each word is spoken a number of times, indicated by small circles that are coloured green when the word has been repeated.

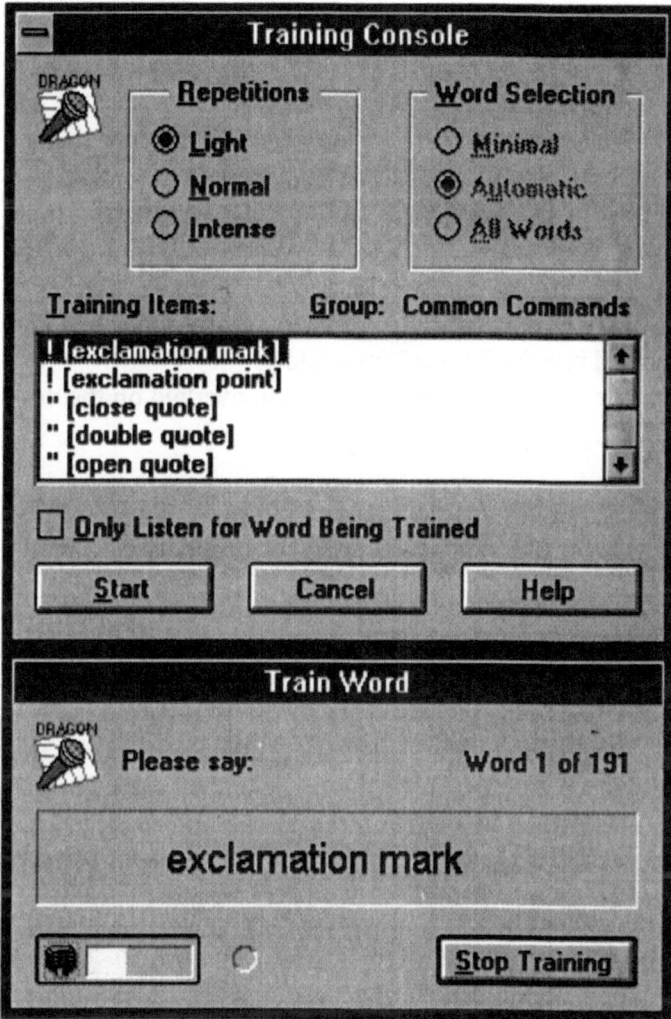

There are three different training intensities. Within these intensities the word is given a minimum or a maximum number of repeats as follows:

light: 1–3
normal: 3–5
intense: 6–8

It is up to the user to choose the intensity. The higher the intensity, the longer this "quick" training takes.

If you have to say more than one word (i.e. when the utterance is a phrase or a command), for example [CHOOSE 10], then say the command as one word *without* a pause between the words.

DRAGONDICTATE FOR WINDOWS AFTER THE INITIAL TRAINING SESSION

If you want the package to come up each time you enter Windows, copy the icon to the "Start-up" folder on your desktop. To activate the package from the DragonDictate for Windows folder, double-click with the mouse on the icon and DragonDictate for Windows will load.

If you want to be able to activate, say, Word 6 by voice then the Word icon needs to be copied into the DragonDictate folder.

You will notice that at the top of the screen, overlaid on the desktop, is the VoiceBar.

The commands that you have just trained can now be used. If you are in the DragonDictate folder you can move the focus (i.e. the highlighting) using speech. If you say [MOVE RIGHT] the focus will move to the right.

The VoiceBar tells you the current state of the speech system. The Voice Menu button lets you choose menu commands. The next box shows you the active vocabulary. The microphone button is coloured green when it is "on" and grey when it is "off". The Last Word box gives the last word that the system thinks you uttered.

If you move the focus to the Word 6 icon and say [BRING UP] [MICROSOFT WORD] the Word package will be loaded. The active vocabulary will change to the Word vocabulary. As the Word vocabulary is loaded it means that you can now say [FILE] [NEW] to create a new document window. (Although this is not necessary, because Word creates a new document window when it first loads up.)

To change the vocabulary to the Dictation vocabulary, so that you can dictate some text, you say [DICTATE MODE]. This give you access to almost 30 000 ordinary words, which you can now dictate.

If you now say the word "thank" the program will look through the 30 000 dictation vocabulary and filter out a match for the utterance. The "best" choice, by recognition factor and the statistical count of the word, is put into the text. The other possible choices are displayed in a "Choice list" at the top right of the screen.

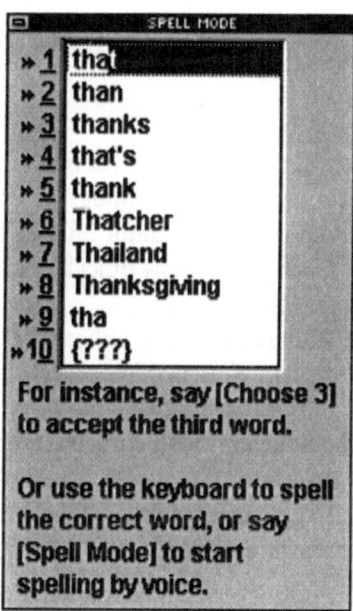

In this case the program put the word "that" into the document but the word "thank" appeared in the "Choice list" as number 5. You say [CHOOSE 5] to get the word "that" replaced by the word "thank".

If the word you said does not appear on the screen, then you say [SPELL MODE] and start to either type out the word or spell it out using the phonetic alphabet. As you type the opening characters of the word, the choices in the "Choice list" gradually change until the word you require is displayed in full and can be exchanged for the wrong word in the text.

The system "learns" by this method, because it is permanently in learn mode. Saying a word and then correcting it once will alter your speech pattern for that word. The next time you say the same word, the system may get it right or it may need to be corrected yet again before the speech pattern for that word has been completely changed to the way you say it. When in spell mode, you can instruct the system to train a new word three times before it replaces it in the text. This obviously make the recognition of the word much more certain the second time.

The entry of text using this method is quite slow at first because a large percentage of words do need to be corrected. The further your voice is from the "mean" voice, the more you will need to correct the system. This percentage correction gets better and better as the system is used but a fair amount of perseverance is needed at the beginning.

The next chapter interviews users who have gone through this process, and shows that they have had dedication in pioneering this new technology. None of those whom I spoke to had anything but praise for the results they are getting from speech activation.

ADDING NEW WORDS OR PHRASES TO DRAGONDICTATE FOR WINDOWS

Most of the common words that you will use will be in the 30 000 vocabulary. When you are typing out a word in spell mode the program searches the 30 000 speech pattern first and then, if it cannot find the word, it searches the large 120 000 dictionary. It is surprising how quickly the word is found, often after entering only the first two characters.

If the word you have just uttered is not in either of these two vocabularies then you will have to type the complete word because the system will run out of guesses. In this case it is essential that you then say [TRAIN WORD] to ensure that the word is adequately trained because there will not be any prior "mean" speech pattern for this word.

The 30 000 vocabulary is the maximum that can be handled by the system, so when you add a new word, the program looks through the existing vocabulary and removes a word that you have never uttered and that has a low statistical usage word count.

Theoretically, this means that you could replace all 30 000 words in the user's speech pattern with a complete set of new words. This is very different to the IBM system, which has a 30 000 completely fixed vocabulary and only 2000 extra words that are replaceable, giving a possible total of 32 000. Note, however, that both Dragon and IBM offer a bigger vocabulary system (60 000 words) and both are now offering add-on specialized vocabularies for certain businesses.

It also has to be remembered that the bigger the vocabulary, the lower the recognition rate. The statistic for the normal business person uttering between 4000 and 6000 different words in a whole year's correspondence rather makes these gigantic vocabularies redundant. There is obviously a place for large vocabulary systems with authors and journalists, but for most business people and executives, who originate standard business letters, the small or medium-sized vocabulary, with its near 99% recognition accuracy, is perfectly adequate.

The entry of phrases into DragonDictate for Windows is the same as entering words. However, at the time of going to press, Dragon do not offer any preset phrase vocabulary, so if you are entering phrases these will have to be typed or entered using the phonetic alphabet. There is a technique to enter individual words into a phrase by speaking them in. This facility becomes a bit tricky if you have not already got most of the individual words being recognized as close to the 95% rate as possible.

The reason for this is that if you say a word and the system gets it wrong, then you are into two corrections overlaid on top of each other. The handling of this becomes very complicated indeed.

In fact, the error correction of DragonDictate for Windows is very time consuming, especially when the user is just learning how to use the system. One user who had used both OfficeSpeak Lite and DragonDictate for Windows commented on the fact that the Lite was much more robust. With the Dragon system, if you make a mistake or a series of mistakes you must correct all of the mistakes that have occurred. The system is learning all the time, so if you do not correct it, your speech pattern will get muddied and the recognition will go to pot. With OfficeSpeak Lite the system only learns when you are entering the word for the first time or if you purposely go back and retrain, which happens very infrequently. The rest of the time it does not matter if the system makes a mistake: you can simply wipe the garbage from the screen.

To get around this problem, Dragon have built what is termed the "Word History" buffer. If you have made more than one mistake in recognition you say [OOPS] and this buffer is displayed.

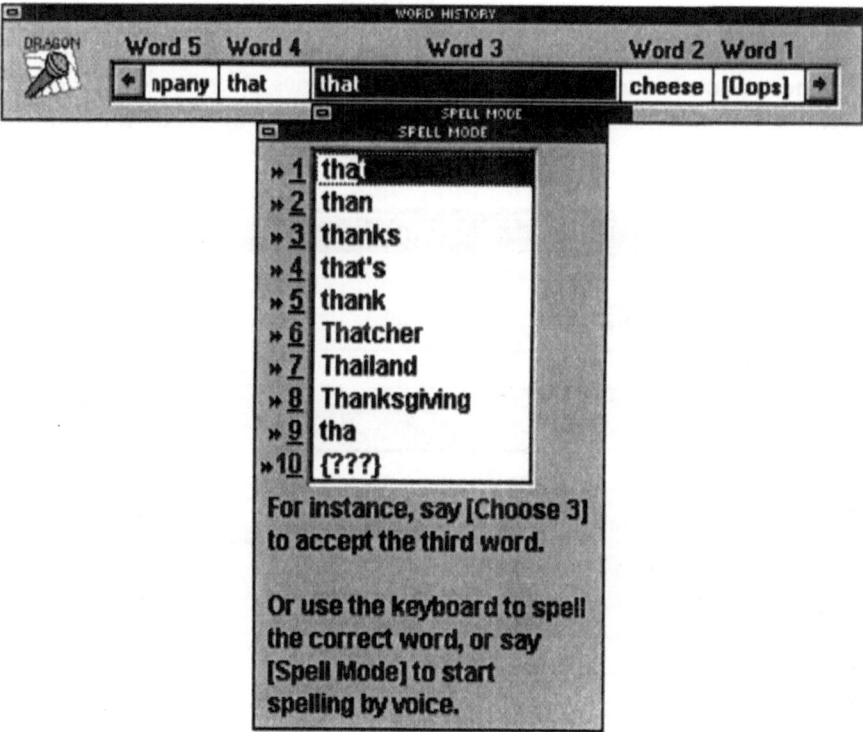

Using this buffer you can clean up the words and, therefore, keep your speech pattern pure.

OPERATING WITH COMMANDS USING DRAGONDICTATE FOR WINDOWS

DragonDictate for Windows is a WYSIWYG package. This means that when you are dictating a letter the phrases go straight into the word processing package you are using, in real time.

In DragonDictate for Windows the user operates in real time all of the time, even when performing commands. For example, if you want to go into bold text you say [FONT BOLD], which operates a macro that presses {Ctrl+b} to embolden all text that follows. To turn off the bold font you repeat the command.

Note that the bold hotkey {Ctrl+b} is a toggle. If repeating the above command is not natural enough, you can define two commands, [BOLD ON] and [BOLD OFF], which both send the {Ctrl+b} key combination.

To enter a command you say the word and then say [SPELL MODE]. When the choice list appears you type in the command as [BOLD ON]: the convention is that commands are contained in square brackets and are normally put in upper case.

Connected to each command there must be a series of keystrokes, called a macro. When you press {Enter} or say [OK] a dialogue opens up for you to enter the macro.

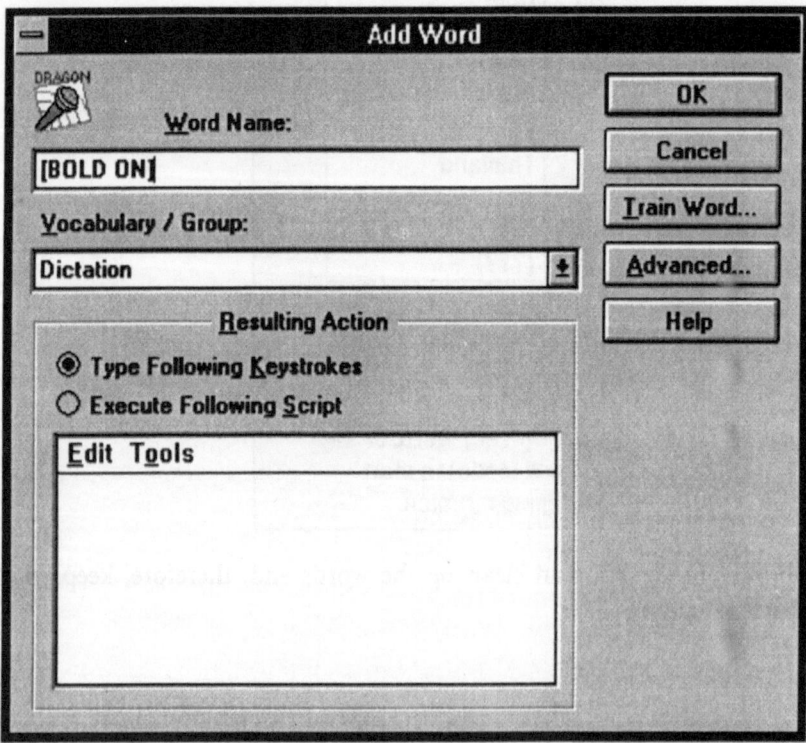

If you do not attach a macro (called an "action" by Dragon) to a command and try to exit from the dialogue you will get an error message to that effect. To enter the macro you click the "Tools" menu choice and press {Ctrl+b} to get it to appear in the action box. When the macro has been entered the command should be trained like any ordinary word or phrase.

Once the command has been trained it can be used in real time to move smoothly from regular font to bold font.

WORKING WITH VOCABULARIES WITH DRAGONDICTATE FOR WINDOWS

Dragon have built into DragonDictate for Windows the concept of "tracking". This is their way of handling the layers of dialogues that you get in an application such as Microsoft Word. You can go into command mode by saying [COMMAND MODE], then the package will "track" where you are in the menu system. You could then say [FILE] [PRINT] [OK] to print a document. At each stage of working through the dialogues the tracking system keeps a note of which dialogue you are in and what you can say in each dialogue.

To view this tracking you can display the active vocabularies in the Vocabulary Manager directly by saying [WHAT CAN I SAY]. The Vocabulary Manager shows the vocabularies that you are currently connected to and the words, phrases and commands that you can say at that moment.

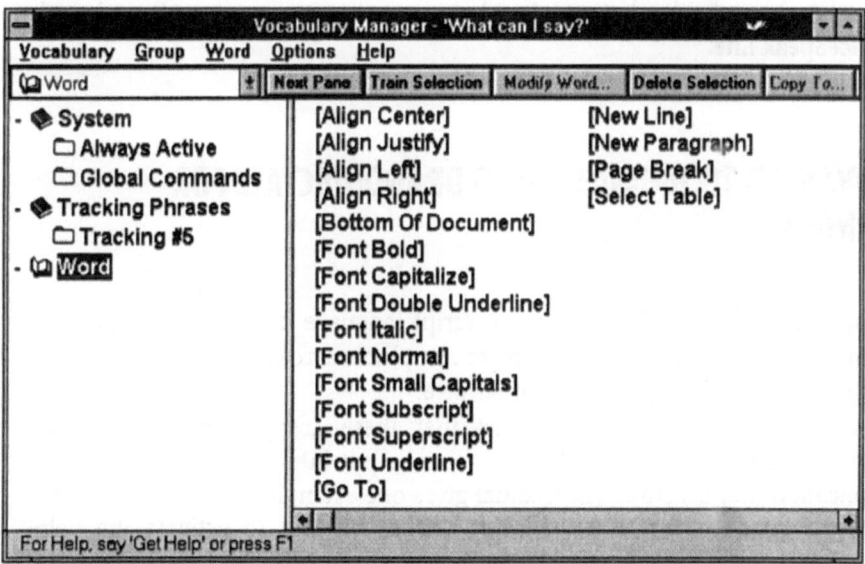

The tracking supplied by Dragon handles the Windows desktop programs, such as File Manager, the Microsoft Office Suite (but not Access) and the following packages:

- Lotus 123
- AmiPro
- cc Mail 2.0
- CrossTalk
- Microsoft Mail
- Paradox
- ProComm Plus
- WordPerfect 6.0

You can view all of these vocabularies by clicking on the Voice Menu button and selecting Vocabulary Manager.

In real terms this tracking is only really useful for people with disabilities, because it gives complete hands-free operation for these users. Most other users will use their mouse to get to menu items because it is quicker and easier to do so.

In the Dragon system you can build commands that reside in the Dictation vocabulary, which will do the normal functions that are required by the user. In this way the package is very similar to the macro facility of OfficeSpeak Lite.

These macros can be exported to an external file then imported into another user's speech pattern. This is done by menu selection. A complete vocabulary needs to be taken across to the new user; there is no selected command exchange, either between vocabularies or between users, as there is with OfficeSpeak Lite.

ADVANCED TECHNIQUES USING DRAGONDICTATE FOR WINDOWS

Dragon have built a comprehensive script language into DragonDictate for Windows. This enables a user to create complex macros that can do a series of instructions just by speaking one utterance.

In their manual Dragon suggest that these are put into the Global Commands vocabulary, but they can also be put into the vocabulary of the application that is active. The manual gives one example but does not list the script commands that are available. The user needs to activate the help function from the menu, type "Script", then choose "Scripting Language" to get the full list.

CONCLUSION ON DRAGONDICTATE FOR WINDOWS

We hope that the above summary gives a good idea about how you would operate the package. The executives whom we have interviewed who have used the package say that it took quite some effort to get this package to a point where they felt that it operated well for them.

Having said that, it is probably the best large vocabulary package on the market at present, and it is the obvious choice for any user who wants to create varied documents or write a book.

Example Speech Packages: Series Editor's Notes

The accounts given of example packages assume that the user has access to personal computer, keyboard and mouse. Typical applications include driving Windows software, such as Microsoft Word, from speech. Arguably, established users of Windows software are finding current interface technology adequate for their needs. Speech activation may be attractive to those now contemplating conversion from DOS.

Conversion to speech activation is likely to require an element of initial consultancy support, with some assurance of ongoing access to advice and upgrades. This becomes more practical as the technology stabilizes, and relations between the leading vendors become more mature. Support needs will vary in different application fields.

Speech is primarily a means of communication between people, and it will be human support that is critical. Just as speech therapists help with the resolution of problems of speech and language, we will need new skilled professionals to help with the computer applications of speech. Their role will be like that of knowledge engineers in the building of knowledge based systems, understanding the problems and needs of users in their specialist areas, and enabling them to express themselves in terms that the technology can recognize.

For some technical specialists, such help in clear expression may be seen as long overdue, and more than a matter of interacting with computers. Computers provide a stimulus to us to reflect on our problems and practices, and to communicate to good effect. Speech can indeed be an action.

There are dangers. What happens if the pace of technological change continues, and investment in learning particular systems is not maintained? Who is to enforce standards across the growing market of competing products, on offer to an undiscerning public? Can we assume that user who have gained experience on a relatively simple product can transfer their experience and skills to a new system in their own institution, or with partners?

Case Studies 5

Introduction

In this chapter I am going to describe interviews I have conducted with five different users of speech recognition software. Each of these users was using a different speech product, and they had vastly different circumstances. The case studies are as follows:

Case study 1: Director of international interior design contractors using CADSpeak for Windows.

Case study 2: Senior partner from a small London firm of solicitors using DragonDictate Classic.

Case study 3: RSI sufferer using Shakespeare DOS SpeechWriter.

Case study 4: Partially sighted trust manager from a large London firm of solicitors using OfficeSpeak Lite.

Case study 5: IT coordinator from a major UK bank using the IBM PDS.

Case Study 1: Director of International Interior Design Contractors Using CADSpeak for Windows

HOW DID YOU COME TO BE USING SPEECH RECOGNITION PRODUCTS?

Our company has a team of designers and cost engineers whom I have endeavoured to move from manual methods to computers. We had staff who were vastly experienced in their job but had no knowledge of computers. In general, I consider that computers are too complicated, and I have always tried to make the introduction of computers as easy for the staff as possible.

I have even had specialized costing software written so that we can place, say, a piece of furniture on a drawing in AutoCad, and have the costing automatically appear in the specification schedule.

I saw speech activation as a way of eliminating complicated key combinations and replacing them with simple spoken commands. I wanted a front end on AutoCad so that the operators could, for example, say:

[23 LEVER STREET] [ROOM 23] [ADD SETTEE]

This would load up the correct job without having to mention a job number, because staff hate numbers, especially large stock or job numbers. The correct room drawing would then appear on the screen, and then the operator could add a settee to the drawing by saying [ADD SETTEE] and clicking the mouse at the position it should be placed.

I wanted my staff to talk to the computer fairly normally, and be able to operate without having to learn all the computer jargon that I have had to learn over the last five years.

HOW DID YOU MAKE YOUR CHOICE OF PRODUCT?

I reviewed three products in my search for the speech recognition I required. The IBM Personal Dictation System at the time I looked was only under OS/2, and as we are essentially Windows-based that was ruled out. Also, the IBM is not WYSIWYG and was therefore unsuitable for a more "command-driven" application, which I was looking for.

The DragonDictate Classic system was WYSIWYG and could have been used to drive the applications that I required. I saw some demonstrations of the system, and was not impressed with the recognition rate. The manufacturers quoted me 94% recognition efficiency but the demonstration I saw, even from an "expert", was not up to that standard.

I went to a "briefing" on the OfficeSpeak products and the recognition rate was first class. It was 100%, actually, but Shakespeare do not claim that statistic. They went to the trouble of explaining the differences between the three packages.

I was not put off by the fact that there were only 900 words in each vocabulary because in reality we only use about 10% of the commands in AutoCad and that does not amount to many commands at all.

The Vocabulary Manager, and the ease of entering new commands and their macros, was much easier and more understandable than the DragonDictate product. I was able to put together the commands and phrases that we require for our operation. Using the export facility provided in the package I could then pass these new vocabularies to my staff and, 20 minutes later, after training the commands, they are up and operating with them.

HOW HAS SPEECH ACTIVATION AFFECTED YOUR BUSINESS?

We are still working at getting both computerization and speech recognition widely used in the company. I see it as the only way to make us more efficient and competitive. I have already been able to save on staff by automating the drawing to estimating cost stages of our product.

Speech activation has allowed us to retain the really experienced people we have, who would have normally floundered with the introduction of computers.

Case Study 2: Senior Partner from Small London Solicitors Using DragonDictate Classic

HOW DID YOU COME TO BE USING SPEECH RECOGNITION PRODUCTS?

I first saw the voice recognition program being demonstrated at the Legal and Solicitors Exhibition at the Barbican. I have a small two-partner practice with two secretaries. Both my partner and I were finding ourselves frustrated at not being able to do things ourselves because we couldn't type. Quite often we would be working late after the secretaries had gone home, and it was like having your hands tied behind your back.

HOW DID YOU MAKE YOUR CHOICE OF PRODUCT?

Up to that point we were in the ark as far as computer equipment was concerned, and only one of the secretaries had a very old word processing machine. We approached a dealer and they recommended a four-user network, with Microsoft Word and OfficeSpeak Lite as the speech package.

It was a bit traumatic at first because we had to learn about computers, about Windows, about Microsoft Word and about the speech package. It was a very early and restricted version of OfficeSpeak Lite, before it upgraded to 36 vocabularies, but we did get the hang of talking to the computer, and the front end is definitely easier for a beginner at computers.

The dealer felt after we had been operational for two months that it would be beneficial to upgrade to DragonDictate Classic Edition for Windows. In hindsight, with the increased capability of the new OfficeSpeak Lite, we might not have changed, but at the time it seemed a wise choice. I do not regret that move because, being a small practice, we originate a wide range of documents and we are not very specialized.

However, the Dragon product is far more complicated to use and is far less robust than OfficeSpeak Lite. You have to correct any mistake you make in DragonDictate, whereas in OfficeSpeak Lite it does not matter because it only learns when you train a word. We have tended to drop back to "dalek speak", because essentially we are lazy.

We have put in a few phrases, and the recognition is far better using Phrase Technology but because DragonDictate already has the "mean speech patterns for the 30 000 individual words" loaded we just tend to dictate on a word for word basis.

I think that those who persevere with OfficeSpeak Lite, and enter in all their phrases will have a much more efficient system and much better recognition, but the system we are now using is very workable. It is far better than having no system, although it did take us a couple of months to get up to speed.

HOW HAS SPEECH ACTIVATION AFFECTED YOUR BUSINESS?

It has allowed us to become independent and not reliant on the whims of our secretarial staff. We have been using it for six months now and we definitely do more work. We do not interrupt the secretaries so much and so they do more work as well. I would estimate that we are 15% at least more efficient than before.

I think it has to be said that putting in the computer network generally has been a major part of this new efficiency, but without speech activation we would never have embarked upon this venture in the first place. We bought the complete system through a lease deal, so it has not affected our cashflow too much, and I would say that it is already paying for itself.

It gives me a lot of personal satisfaction to dictate my letters. I think you get a better quality of work. It is better than using a Dictaphone because you can immediately see what you have said, and you can correct it easily without having to fiddle around rewinding the tape.

Personally, I think that speech activation is the best breakthrough our profession has seen in the last 10 years.

Case Study 3: RSI Sufferer Using Shakespeare DOS SpeechWriter

HOW DID YOU COME TO BE USING SPEECH RECOGNITION PRODUCTS?

I had worked as a secretary for nine years, typing at a rate of 90 words per minute. I started to get very bad pains in my hands and arms. It became so painful that I couldn't even hold a pen in my hand to write normally. I had to give up work.

I decided that I would do a BA degree for primary school teaching, and get away from the keyboard for ever. The problem was that I had to do my degree course and write essays etc. and I could not even hold a pen. I had a friend who also had RSI, who had heard about the SpeechWriter.

HOW DID YOU MAKE YOUR CHOICE OF PRODUCT?

I travelled to the Compatibility Centre in the Midlands to talk to them about my problem. They recommended various speech systems that were available on the market. My friend was connected with a computer dealer in London and they thought the best on the market at the time was the SpeechWriter, which was a 20 000 large vocabulary DOS system.

I got funding through a government agency and just ordered the complete system. It took a bit of learning but I was able to write essays without having to use my hands at all.

HOW HAS SPEECH ACTIVATION AFFECTED YOUR LIFE?

I would not have been able to do my course without the SpeechWriter. It has enabled me to do all my college assignments. I have even started writing children's stories and plays. It has been a boon.

I have to speak like a dalek with this system, and that is a bit annoying and a bit unnatural but at least I am able to get the words onto the screen. I want to upgrade to the Windows version of the program, but I would have to start training my speech patterns from scratch and that is a daunting thought now that it is working OK for me. Also, it costs money, and as a student I am not exactly flush.

I rather like the idea of speaking in phrases because I find dalek speak, as I said before, to be tedious. Also, I have asked if it is possible to have a desktop microphone rather than a headset one. I understand that the problem with a desktop microphone is that we naturally move our head around and the recognition goes down. The only other solution is to buy a very costly wireless headset mic that allows you to walk around the room with no wires attached. That and a six foot square flat screen on the wall would do me fine, but I think I am dreaming.

In conclusion, I would say that, for any secretary with any signs of RSI, I recommend that you insist your company moves you over to speech recognition systems. To continue using a keyboard, and get the suffering I went through, is really criminal.

Case Study 4: Partially Sighted Trust Manager from Large London Solicitors Using OfficeSpeak Lite

HOW DID YOU COME TO BE USING SPEECH RECOGNITION PRODUCTS?

I had read about speech recognition in the computer magazines but it was the BBC Radio 4 program *Word of Mouth* about OfficeSpeak Lite that prompted me to buy the package.

I am partially sighted, so when I am using my computer I have to be about two inches from the screen to see the words. This actually is not that much of an inconvenience but I am not a touch typist and therefore I have spent the last four years bending close to the keyboard, and that has really done my back in. I thought that if I could just speak in my work, then I could straighten up again and relieve my back problems.

HOW DID YOU MAKE YOUR CHOICE OF PRODUCT?

I do many administrative and accountancy tasks in the practice and therefore I am chopping and changing between many applications, so it was essential that the speech program was able to carry out commands on a real-time basis. This ruled out the IBM product, which is essentially only for dictation of large chunks of text and uses a window into which you dictate your text before transferring to the application you are using.

I chose OfficeSpeak Lite over the Dragon product because it was less likely to make a mistake, because it searches only 900 words instead of 29 000. As I need, for example, to jump from Excel to Word and back many times in the course of a day, it was essential that, if I gave the command, I did not end up in Solitaire, especially if one of the partners was present!

The small amount of word processing that I do consists of about 20% standard letters, and about 80% more varied letters. Now that I am beginning to master speaking to my computer, I am thinking of getting the Dragon-Dictate product and using both of them: OfficeSpeak Lite for the majority of my work and DragonDictate Classic for Windows for whenever I have to dictate a more varied letter.

I am only just getting into using Phrase Technology, and time will have to tell if it is adequate for all my word processing work, or whether the dual system idea will have to be implemented.

HOW HAS SPEECH ACTIVATION AFFECTED YOUR WORK?

It is certainly helping to mend my back.

I am beginning to see how using voice is making tasks more easy and quicker. I still use the mouse a lot but I can do that without having to look at it, as I have to with the keyboard.

The more I use speech, the more I see possibilities for use. I am very impressed with what it does.

I am working on the partner who is responsible for IT in the practice to implement speech systems with the fee earning partners. Already some of the partners are getting notebooks for doing work at home. It is not such a large step for them to speech activate these notebooks. In fact, it would make their learning curve into computer use much easier, faster and more enjoyable.

Case Study 5: IT Coordinator from Major UK Bank Using the IBM PDS

HOW DID YOU COME TO BE USING SPEECH RECOGNITION PRODUCTS?

It is my job to be aware of the IT technologies that are coming onto the market, to understand them, and to make a judgement about whether they should be implemented in the bank.

I had been discussing speech recognition with the head of my legal department, who had seen a demonstration at the Legal and Solicitors Exhibition.

I had a reseller demonstrate both the DragonDictate product and OfficeSpeak Lite. I also had the IBM PDS system under OS/2 demonstrated to me.

My decision to buy really came when I lost my secretary, who was replaced by an admin assistant who could not type.

My work consists of making fairly long reports of a varied nature and so a large vocabulary system was essential. So, it was choice between the IBM system and the DragonDictate system. At the time Dragon had not completed their Windows version, and so I decided to go for the IBM system.

HOW DID YOU MAKE YOUR CHOICE OF PRODUCT?

I was very impressed by the way the IBM system did context analysis and changed the words after doing that analysis. As the words appearing on the screen tend to lag behind my speech, I find I do not look at the screen when dictating a letter. I only look at what is coming up if I am examining the analysis process for scientific interest.

Some people I have shown the system to do not like the fact that the text is dictated into a separate window, and then has to be transferred into the application and further manipulated for changing font, underlining etc. My argument here is that most of the manipulation work is done with the mouse, and I am happy to do that as I would if I was typing it.

The other advantage is that I can dictate fairly rapidly, even though I admit in a dalek fashion, without having to correct anything until my flow has stopped. Then I go back and correct the mistakes. It is between 85% and 95% efficient, so there are quite a few corrections to be made. As I have used the system, this has got better. Nowadays, in a short one-page letter I correct about six words. This recognition rate is acceptable to me, even if other staff don't think it is good enough.

HOW HAS SPEECH ACTIVATION AFFECTED YOUR COMPANY?

I myself couldn't operate without speech now, but it is a very difficult decision to order this new technology into the bank. I feel, from the reaction I have had from the staff around me, that there would be resistance to its implementation.

It is a question of what is acceptable to the individual staff member. Most of the staff I have shown it to are intrigued by it, of course. The recognition rate can be quite frustrating, especially at the outset before it improves. Also, speaking in individual words puts off a lot of staff.

I have only got two converts, both in the legal department, who have taken up the technology to date, and I have had my system for almost a year. IBM have just re-issued the system under Windows with the new name IBM VoiceType. Being under Windows makes it easier to implement in the bank.

I think for verbose legal work and IT reports the IBM system is ideal. I suspect that wide use of voice recognition in the bank will have to wait for word recognition improvements, but then each of the major player's offerings seems to improve on each release, and I personally don't think it will be long before the staff will be demanding speech systems rather than us pioneers trying to force it down their throats.

Case Studies: Series Editor's Notes

The case study approach is important and illuminating, and provides a useful counterbalance to high pressure sales talk. It is important that case studies are not simply undertaken by vendors who start with the clear objective of selling a particular product. The introduction of speech technology can have complex implications for the organization and the culture of the workplace: we need a practical, collaborative and multidisciplinary approach.

KINGSTON BUSINESS SCHOOL

The Kingston Business School experience demonstrates that proof of the effective working of the technology does not necessarily mean that the technology is taken up and diffused. An excellent demonstration by company staff from Shakespeare SpeechWriter Ltd convinced senior university technical staff that the technology was viable, and a further presentation motivated students and teaching staff.

However, the time taken in training with the SpeechWriter package then available on DOS, and the fact that it required additional specialist hardware, meant that the system did not impact on the institution much beyond attaining the status of an effective demonstration of what could be done. The first system was tailored to a proprietary word processor rather than the in-house standard, WordPerfect, although a second system provided speech activation for WordPerfect. SpeechWriter also became available for DOS at the time when the opinion formers in the university were moving on to the use of Windows.

Information technology is an unforgiving market-place in which to sell: standards move on at speed, and fierce competition reduces profit margins, making many forms of traditional consultancy no longer viable. This makes it difficult for small new entrants to the market, dealing with single products.

This is not to say that the SpeechWriter product was ineffective. A group of students, engaged in a consultancy project on speech-driven computers, developed a speech-driven implementation of Lotus 1-2-3. The user would need to understand the conventional Lotus spreadsheet, but would be freed from using the keyboard. For many users this is of limited attraction, because the keyboard does not present major problems for them. It could, however, prove invaluable for those who need to maintain accounts but are disabled, or new to the use of computers.

The technology comes into its own when it is being used to perform an actual task, rather than just as an experimental plaything. One task was to support a lecture on new technology and business ethics at London Business School, where a live audience were interested primarily in the subject, and only secondarily in the means of delivery.

EXTERNAL CONSULTANCY WITH SPEECH-DRIVEN SYSTEMS

Extended work with major external clients has unearthed other issues.

In the world of high technology, dealers may not be users. Technology transfer is inevitably a problem for computer dealers. Their primary purpose in acquiring new products is to sell them at a profit, and use "in anger" is not their direct concern. When they offer a demonstration, they may be unable to go beyond the example and script provided. The key missing link is extended practice supported by the technology. This takes time, and depends on both success among pioneering users and effective means of communication of results and conclusions.

University-based consultants have been able to explore the potential of the technology with prospective clients, who were often discouraged once they realized the training overhead that was then involved even for senior users. Large organizations, such as the police or health services, may appoint staff to investigate new technologies, but they do not usually provide them with budgets to support serious implementation.

Demonstrations of the technology to potential clients need to be in terms of recognizably appropriate examples and styles of use. The language, idiom and modes of communication need to have a familiar ring. One standard demonstration is unlikely to suffice. Thus, a demonstration for a major multinational organization will need to be different from that for a small business. Defence manufacturers (such as British Aerospace) will have different needs from retail chains (such as Marks and Spencer). The audiences will vary, with different people who need to be convinced and empowered to make the next move. As demand rises from different potential users, it is unrealistic to suppose that a small company has the resources to meet all the needs. In British Aerospace an investigation was made of the potential for speech activation of the Computer Aided Wiring Diagrams (BCAWD) package. The researcher, Peter Whitney, was a former British Aerospace manager of the BCAWD project, completing a business information technology degree at Kingston Business School. He thus brought domain expertise and company credibility, together with knowledge of speech activation and problems of technology transfer. Users of the conventional BCAWD system have been electrical design engineers, draughtsmen and avionic engineers, with skills in their specialist areas and long experience of use of a drawing board. They are designers rather than computer scientists, and can feel intimidated by what appears to be complex technology. A customized speech interface might help to allay some of their worries, removing their fear that they could somehow break the system. Although a demonstration of speech technology provided convincing evidence of the viability of the technology, experimental work is needed in the design office environment to determine whether interference from background noise would be a problem, and whether modifications to the layout of the office would impair the effectiveness of the team.

There is reason to believe that speech can enhance the work of designers. The Shakespeare CADSpeak system has enabled the AutoCad user to drive the software by speech rather than from the keyboard: the mouse, although a powerful desktop device, should not have to be used at the same time for drawing and for selecting tools. The case for the individual user using speech appears strong; experimental trials will help us to understand the organizational dimension.

Here we may meet an insuperable set of obstacles. A major multinational organization may have established common practices and procedures, and may be intolerant of experimentation. Budgetary responsibilities may have been devolved, but with little freedom to undertake workplace-based experimental research and development at local level.

Peter Whitney also worked within Marks and Spencer, following some months of temporary employment in the company. He identified potential areas of application of speech technology, focusing on the General Stock Adjustment–Multi User Warehouse system, especially with regard to return to manufacturers. Individuals needed to be able to record the necessary data while performing the physical task of sorting and packaging items for return. He identified a finite vocabulary that was needed, and secured access to the code of the software system concerned. This did not lead to a magic solution. The software had been developed in an unstructured manner, with little documentation available within the user company, who relied on the external supplier for maintenance and support. Although it appeared technically feasible to link SpeechWriter software with the return to manufacturer system, ongoing changes in that system and different priorities on the part of Marks and Spencer meant that the system was not built.

Development of a speech-driven interface to an active application requires access to technical documentation, but increasingly companies have outsourced their IT requirements from external suppliers, and have neither control over, nor documentation for, what were their own systems. The outsourcing contractors are keen to retain unimpaired control, as this protects their future revenue stream. They are uninterested in experimental implementations using new technology that do not offer a guarantee of assured high levels of return in the short term.

EUROPEAN PASSENGER SERVICES

With new systems of rail transport through the Channel Tunnel expanding rapidly, providing links between previously unconnected cities, new services are required, coping with customers speaking diverse languages. It could be appropriate to install new speech-driven systems for European Passenger Services (EPS) telesales staff concerned with the Eurostar train service, enabling them to offer a greater range of services.

Rather than the caller communicating with a speech-activation system, the telesales staff would use head microphones and the Windows software environment during calls.

Where EPS became involved in associated activities, such as an international festival using their transport facilities, telesales staff would have automatic access to data maintained under Windows systems, including hotel reservation systems and package holiday information.

"Phrase speak" would be applicable, as key phrases in either French or English could be used to drive the software applications. The key to success would be expert consultancy from within EPS, identifying the phrases most often used by staff and the principal information processing needs.

MANAGING HEALTH: AFTER THE REFORMS

The reformed National Health Service in the UK faces a number of bureaucratic challenges for which computers have to date failed to find a full solution. Recent demonstrations of speech-activated systems to senior health service managers have excited considerable interest, and 10 evaluation systems are being installed. It is not difficult to understand the interest.

Managers need to know more about official practices for prescriptions and for patient referrals and discharges, if official statistics are to be more than meaningless palliatives. There needs to be a consistent mode of recording information, and monitoring of details of medicines prescribed, together with maintenance of patient records. The vocabulary concerned is known, and precision can be a matter of life and death. It could be attractive to introduce systems that will recognize and act on approved instructions, authorizing prescriptions, for example, only of medicines on the official list.

Many doctors have failed to use computers, despite their availability, and thus records become inconsistent. In a typical general practice one or two of the partners may be enthusiastic computer users, giving up some of their own time to use and develop the system, but others have declared that the keyboard and screen represent an unwanted barrier between the doctor and the patient. An appropriate speech-driven system could enable doctors and other health professionals to follow official practices.

GOOD PARTICIPATIVE PRACTICE

Can we point to examples of good practice in involving staff in the introduction of new speech technology, including job and office design?

Is it important to define a core vocabulary of words and phrases that capture the essence of the culture of the organization? How can this be done?

The technology is new, but the issue of workplace participation is long established.

QUESTIONS

There will be questions:

- Can I switch to speech activation of my current applications software?
- Will this be straightforward, or will radical redesign be necessary to ensure that the applications are "speech safe"?
- Have the relevant speech software packages and environments stabilized, or is any investment likely to be repeated in the near future?
- When should we expect systems to be delivered with speech activation as a standard option, together with mouse?

In some cases we can see the issue emerging of using speech technology to replace staff. We need to reflect on the nature of the skills of those whose jobs are threatened, and the extent to which the new technology can deal with that skill element:

- What sort of jobs are threatened?
- Who needs to know what in order to ensure effective implementation of speech-driven systems?

We may be at the early stages of a technological revolution in the workplace. Mistakes could prove expensive.

Products on the Market Now

6

Introduction

In this chapter I am going to describe the products that you can buy right now from your local dealer. I have divided these by vocabulary size so that you can get a better idea of like for like packages. I have also introduced products from some of the smaller manufacturers, although you may not so easily find dealers who know anything about these products.

There is also a plethora of "tiny vocabulary" systems growing up for telephony. This is an area of speech recognition that has exploded over the past few years. Most of these systems are for inclusion in a company's telephone system boxes and not for use on a computer and therefore are not discussed here. This will change over the next five years, as most telephone dialling will be done from the desktop computer, and telephones in business as we know them today will die out.

This list of speech-recognition products will be out of date even before this book hits the bookshops. There is nothing we can do about this; the computer industry moves so fast. It may be that books of this nature will within five years be available via cable and read on the screen. If that was the case then a factual book of this nature could be updated weekly. Perish the thought!

My advice to the executive who is making a decision about speech recognition after reading this book is to contact your local dealer, buy in a low cost speech system and get your hands dirty. Then, armed with knowledge from this book and some first-hand experience with talking to your computer, you will be in a good position to discuss with a selection of resellers the merits of the latest products appearing on the market.

Very Large Vocabulary

DRAGONDICTATE POWER EDITION FOR WINDOWS

This is Dragon's very large vocabulary system consisting of an active vocabulary of 60 000 words and a reference dictionary of 120 000 words with built-in acoustic models. It is WYSIWYG and completely hands-free, and so can be used by a person with disabilities.

It requires 12 Mb of dedicated RAM on top of normal system requirements. It will operate on a 486 33 MHz or faster personal computer, under Microsoft Windows 3.1 or 3.11. It requires 30 Mb minimum of hard disk storage.

It requires a certified DSP audio board, such as the Techmar ACPA board, or a supported Windows multimedia sound card, such as the Creative Labs Sound Blaster 16 or the Media Vision Pro Audio Studio 16.

The software is supplied on sixteen 3.5 in. 1.44 Mb diskettes. The package includes a "Getting Started Guide", a "User's Guide" and a "Quick Reference Card". It also includes a Shure headset microphone or equivalent.

DRAGONDICTATE POWER EDITION FOR DOS

This has the same specification as the Windows version except that this program operates on the DOS platform instead of Windows. The underlying speech technology is based upon the same algorithm in both cases. The program can only work with an ACPA card.

IBM VOICETYPE DICTATION FOR OS/2 LEGAL VOCABULARY

This is IBM's very large vocabulary system for the legal profession, consisting of an active general vocabulary of 32 000 words with an additional 12 000 legal words. It also has a reference dictionary of 120 000 words with built-in acoustic models. It is not WYSIWYG and dictation is spoken to a "Dictation Window", then transferred later to the word processor you are using. It is, however, completely hands-free, and so can be used by a person with disabilities.

It requires 8 Mb of dedicated RAM on top of normal system requirements.

It will operate on a 486 25 MHz or faster personal computer, under OS/2 2.1 or above. It requires 62 Mb minimum of hard disk storage and an additional 30 Mb during enrolment.

It requires either an IBM special ACPA board or an IBM PCMCIA card.

The software is supplied on sixteen 3.5 in. 1.44 Mb diskettes. The package includes a "Getting Started Guide", a "User's Guide" and a "Quick Reference Card". It also includes a Shure headset microphone or equivalent.

IBM VOICETYPE DICTATION FOR OS/2 RADIOLOGY VOCABULARY

This is IBM's very large vocabulary system for radiologists, consisting of an active general vocabulary of 32 000 words with an additional 6000 radiology words. It also has a reference dictionary of 120 000 words with built-in acoustic models. It is not WYSIWYG and dictation is spoken to a "Dictation Window", then transferred later to the word processor you are using. It is, however, completely hands-free, and so can be used by a person with disabilities or by a professional whose hands are occupied.

It requires 8 Mb of dedicated RAM on top of normal system requirements. It will operate on a 486 25 MHz or faster personal computer, under OS/2 2.1 or above. It requires 48 Mb minimum of hard disk storage and an additional 8 Mb during enrolment.

It requires either an IBM special ACPA board or an IBM PCMCIA card.

The software is supplied on sixteen 3.5 in. 1.44 Mb diskettes. The package includes a "Getting Started Guide", a "User's Guide" and a "Quick Reference Card". It also includes a Shure headset microphone or equivalent.

Large Vocabulary

DRAGONDICTATE CLASSIC EDITION FOR WINDOWS

This is Dragon's large vocabulary system, consisting of an active vocabulary of 30 000 words and a reference dictionary of 120 000 words with built-in acoustic models. It is WYSIWYG and completely hands-free, and so can be used by a person with disabilities.

It requires 12 Mb of dedicated RAM on top of normal system requirements. It will operate on a 486 33 MHz or faster personal computer, under Microsoft Windows 3.1 or 3.11. It requires 20 Mb minimum of hard disk storage.

It requires a certified DSP audio board, such as the Techmar ACPA board, or a supported Windows multimedia sound card, such as the Creative Labs Sound Blaster 16 or the Media Vision Pro Audio Studio 16.

The software is supplied on twelve 3.5 in. 1.44 Mb diskettes. The package includes a "Getting Started Guide", a "User's Guide" and a "Quick Reference Card". It also includes a Shure headset microphone or equivalent.

DRAGONDICTATE CLASSIC EDITION FOR DOS

This has the same specification as the Windows version except that it operates on the DOS platform instead of Windows. The underlying speech technology is based upon the same algorithm in both cases. The program can only work with an ACPA card.

IBM VOICETYPE DICTATION FOR OS/2

This is IBM's large vocabulary system for general dictation, consisting of an active general vocabulary of 32 000 words. It also has a reference dictionary of 120 000 words with built-in acoustic models. It is not WYSIWYG and dictation is spoken to a "Dictation Window", then transferred later to the word processor you are using. It is, however, completely hands-free, and so can be used by a person with disabilities.

It requires 8 Mb of dedicated RAM on top of normal system requirements. It will operate on a 486 25 MHz or faster personal computer, under OS/2 2.1 or above. It requires 32 Mb minimum of hard disk storage and an additional 30 Mb during enrolment.

It requires either an IBM special ACPA board or an IBM PCMCIA card.

The software is supplied on sixteen 3.5 in. 1.44 Mb diskettes. The package includes a "Getting Started Guide", a "User's Guide" and a "Quick Reference Card". It also includes a Shure headset microphone or equivalent.

IBM VOICETYPE DICTATION FOR WINDOWS

This is IBM's large vocabulary system for general dictation on the Windows platform, consisting of an active general vocabulary of 32 000 words. It also has a reference dictionary of 120 000 words with built-in acoustic models. It is not WYSIWYG and dictation is spoken to a "Dictation Window", then transferred later to the word processor you are using. It is, however, completely hands-free.

It requires 12 Mb of dedicated RAM on top of normal system requirements. It will operate on a 486 25 MHz or faster personal computer, under Microsoft Windows 3.1 or 3.11. It requires 40 Mb minimum of hard disk storage and an additional 33 Mb during enrolment.

It requires either an IBM special ACPA board or an IBM PCMCIA card.

The software is supplied on sixteen 3.5 in. 1.44 Mb diskettes. The package includes a "Getting Started Guide", a "User's Guide" and a "Quick Reference Card". It also includes a Shure headset microphone or equivalent.

SHAKESPEARE OFFICESPEAK

This is Shakespeare's large vocabulary system for general operation of all Windows programs, consisting of 99 possible vocabularies with up to 900 words, phrases or commands in each. It accesses to a general 100 000 vocabulary dictionary, a names vocabulary, a place vocabulary and two specialized vocabularies that can be defined by the user. It is WYSIWYG and completely hands-free, and so can be used by a person with disabilities.

It requires 4 Mb of dedicated RAM on top of normal system requirements. It will operate on a 486 33 MHz or faster personal computer, under Microsoft Windows 3.1 or 3.11. It requires 6 Mb minimum of hard disk storage.

It requires a certified DSP audio board, such as the Techmar ACPA board, or a supported Windows multimedia sound card, such as the Creative Labs Sound Blaster 16 or the Media Vision Pro Audio Studio 16.

The software is supplied on three 3.5 in. 1.44 Mb diskettes. The package includes a full manual. It also includes a Shakespeare pressure gradient headset microphone.

KURZVEIL VOICE FOR WINDOWS

This Kurzveil system consists of an active vocabulary of 30 000 words and a reference dictionary of 120 000 words with built-in acoustic models. It is WYSIWYG and completely hands-free, and so can be used by a person with disabilities. There is also a 60 000 version at no extra cost.

It requires 8 Mb of dedicated RAM on top of normal system requirements. It will operate on a 486 33 MHz or faster personal computer, under Microsoft Windows 3.1 or 3.11. It requires 20 Mb minimum of hard disk storage.

The system is supplied with a proprietary full length sound card, which has an on-board DSP chip. It does not support the Windows sound system but is dedicated for speech recognition.

The software is supplied on 3.5 in. 1.44 Mb diskettes, and includes manuals and a headset microphone.

Medium Vocabulary

SHAKESPEARE OFFICESPEAK LITE

This is Shakespeare's medium vocabulary system for general operation of all Windows programs, consisting of 40 possible vocabularies with up to 900 words, phrases or commands in each. It has no access to dictionaries, but vocabulary phrases and commands with macros can be imported into the system. It is WYSIWYG but is not hands-free, and so cannot be used by a person with disabilities.

It requires 2 Mb of dedicated RAM on top of normal system requirements, which means that it will run on an ordinary 8 Mb computer with Windows and an application. It will operate on a 486 33 MHz or faster personal computer, under Microsoft Windows 3.1 or 3.11. It requires 2 Mb minimum of hard disk storage.

It requires a certified DSP audio board, such as the Techmar ACPA board, or a supported Windows multimedia sound card, such as the Creative Labs Sound Blaster 16 or the Media Vision Pro Audio Studio 16.

The software is supplied on two 3.5 in. 1.44 Mb diskettes. The package includes a full manual. It also includes a Shakespeare pressure gradient headset microphone.

DRAGONDICTATE STARTER EDITION FOR WINDOWS

This is Dragon's starter vocabulary system, consisting of an active vocabulary of 5000 words and a reference dictionary of 120 000 words with built-in acoustic models. It is WYSIWYG and completely hands-free, and so can be used by a person with disabilities.

It requires 7 Mb of dedicated RAM on top of normal system requirements. It will operate on a 486 33 MHz or faster personal computer, under Microsoft Windows 3.1 or 3.11. It requires 17 Mb minimum of hard disk storage.

It requires a certified DSP audio board, such as the Techmar ACPA board, or a supported Windows multimedia sound card, such as the Creative Labs Sound Blaster 16 or the Media Vision Pro Audio Studio 16.

The software is supplied on eleven 3.5 in. 1.44 Mb diskettes. The package includes a "Getting Started Guide", a "User's Guide" and a "Quick Reference Card". It also includes a Shure headset microphone or equivalent.

DRAGONDICTATE STARTER EDITION FOR DOS

This has the same specification as the Windows version except that it operates on the DOS platform instead of Windows. The underlying speech technology is based upon the same algorithm in both cases. The program can only work with an ACPA card.

Small Vocabulary

SHAKESPEARE CADSPEAK FOR WINDOWS

This is Shakespeare's special vocabulary system for the CADCAM profession, which will work with any Windows-based CADCAM programs. It consists of 40 possible vocabularies with up to 900 words, phrases or commands in each.

It has no access to dictionaries, but vocabulary phrases and commands with macros can be imported into the system. It is WYSIWYG but not hands-free, and so cannot be used by a person with disabilities.

It requires 2 Mb of dedicated RAM on top of normal system requirements, which means that it will run on a normal CADCAM terminal without the addition of extra RAM. It will operate on a 486 33 MHz or faster personal computer, under Microsoft Windows 3.1 or 3.11. It requires 2 Mb minimum of hard disk storage.

It requires a certified DSP audio board, such as the Techmar ACPA board, or a supported Windows multimedia sound card, such as the Creative Labs Sound Blaster 16 or the Media Vision Pro Audio Studio 16.

The software is supplied on two 3.5 in. 1.44 Mb diskettes. The package includes a full manual. It also includes a Shakespeare pressure gradient headset microphone.

Tiny Vocabulary

ALPSPEAK

This is ALP's general low-cost speech system specifically for Windows control and simple dictation. It consists of 16 possible vocabularies with up to 50 words, phrases or commands in each. However, further vocabularies can be nested within these, giving, in theory, an unlimited number, dependent only on hard disk space.

It requires very little dedicated RAM because much of the processing takes place in the tower. It will operate on a 486 33 MHz or faster personal computer, under Microsoft Windows 3.1 or 3.11. It requires 2 Mb minimum of hard disk storage.

The package comes with its own "speech tower", which fits onto the parallel port. This tower can only be used for the speech program and has no Sound Blaster features.

The software is supplied on two 3.5 in. 1.44 Mb diskettes. The package includes a full manual. It also includes a headset microphone.

ALPSPEAK FOR AUTOCAD LITE

This is ALP's special speech system specifically for AutoCAD LT, the low-cost AutoCad product. It consists of 16 possible vocabularies, with up to 128 words, phrases or commands in each.

It has no access to dictionaries, but vocabulary phrases and commands with macros can be imported into the system. It is WYSIWYG but not hands-free, and so cannot be used by a person with disabilities.

It requires very little dedicated RAM on top of normal system requirements, which means that it will run on a normal CADCAM terminal without the addition of extra RAM. It will operate on a 486 33 MHz or faster personal computer, under Microsoft Windows 3.1 or 3.11. It requires 2 Mb minimum of hard disk storage.

The package comes with its own "speech tower", which fits onto the parallel port. This tower can only be used for the speech program and has no Sound Blaster features.

The software is supplied on two 3.5 in. 1.44 Mb diskettes. The package includes a full manual. It also includes a headset microphone.

Note: Information can be obtained on all of the packages described above by ringing a helpline, on 01342–316456.

Products on the Market Now: Series Editor's Notes

DEVELOPMENT

- Who are the best people to develop and sell speech-activated systems?
- Where is the research base on which development can build?
- To what extent are future users involved in developing the current generation of products?
- Is there scope for more pre-competitive collaboration?

TECHNOLOGY TRANSFER

- Is it sensible to rely on dealers, whose main concern may be to sell products?
- What alternatives are there? Is this a potential area for involvement by Technology Transfer Centres and Training and Enterprise Councils?
- What expertise is required for successful technology transfer?
- How many people have the necessary expertise in speech technology to make serious contributions to the development and implementation of reliable systems for business? How could this situation be changed?

LONG-TERM PLANNING

- Should speech activation be added to an organization as part of a longer term plan?
- Does this depend on some external long-term financial support?

THE NEXT GENERATION

Further case study work is needed to address the issue of speech activation being incorporated as part of an overall user environment in next generation hardware and software.

- Where will this leave the current range of products?

- Are there issues of upgrading and compatibility?
- Does this discourage purchasers?

NICHE MARKETS

It is worth distinguishing between products aimed at the mass market and those designed to add value to existing specialist systems. There is doubtless an emerging custom and consultancy niche market. Defence clients have long been interested in speech activation. Where does this leave ordinary users and small businesses in the civil economy?

CHANNELS TO MARKET

Given the complexities of language use in different knowledge domains, work is needed on new channels to market for this emerging technology. Systems integrators may wish to offer clients a speech interface to a pre-scribed set of applications.

PROCESSING POWER

Chip vendors, such as Intel, need applications that demand more processing power. Speech activation meets their need. There may be new natural alliances. Speech may be presented as a feature provided by the vendor of the new clever chip, rather than as an additional peripheral feature. This is a matter for marketing decisions.

FREEDOM OF SPEECH?

There could be dangers if, for example, Microsoft incorporated non-trivial speech activation in a future release of Windows. We still understand relatively little about how we use speech, with or without computers.

MARKET TRENDS

Do we know who is buying what, and why? The patterns are changing by the month. If demand takes off, can it be managed?

Research and Development in Speech

7

Introduction

In this chapter we are going to describe some of the more scientific aspects of speech recognition. These topics describe a broader aspect than just the products that are selling now. These subjects have been presented in a manner that, I hope, can be understood by the non-technical reader. The topics are as follows:

1. Major design questions facing speech recognition engineers
2. Microphone technology
3. Sound card technology
4. Database searching and template matching
5. Speech recognition using neural networks
6. The use of artificial intelligence in speech systems

Major Design Questions Facing Speech Recognition Engineers

When talking about the different technologies involved in speech recognition it is useful to outline quickly the six major design decisions faced by speech engineers in the development of a speech system.

SPEAKER-DEPENDENCE VERSUS SPEAKER-INDEPENDENCE

If a speech recognition system is *speaker-dependent* then it has to be trained to react to the voice of each user. As each user trains the system, his or her speech pattern is recorded. Before the user can speak to the computer this speech pattern has to be loaded into memory, so that the recognition will work. The system cannot be used by someone else until they have trained their own speech pattern, and that speech pattern is loaded into memory.

When a system is speaker-dependent it can make use of information about how the individual pronounces specific words. For example, a speaker-dependent system will find it easier to cope with strong accents than a speaker-independent system.

If a system is *speaker-independent*, it is not trained for a specific user, but is designed to work for anybody who walks up to it. A speaker-independent system must have knowledge about how it thinks the "average" person will pronounce a certain word. So far, as research has progressed, speaker-independent systems have been built that will recognize only a very small number of words (12–50 words).

The race is on to produce speaker-independent systems that will cope with much larger vocabularies than these tiny recognition systems.

CONTINUOUS VERSUS DALEK SPEAK

Dalek speak is when a user has to pause between words; *continuous speech* is the way we talk in normal conversation. Traditionally, speech recognition systems use dalek speak; continuous speech is seen as the ultimate goal, and much research effort is being made in that direction.

Philips issued a big press announcement in November 1994 about bringing out a continuous speech system. Philips, of course, have a lot to lose if speech activation catches on: they are major manufacturers of dictating machines, and that whole industry will die as the new speech recognition technology replaces it.

My own opinion is that Philips are scrambling to get some speech-recognition technology onto the market to sell to their existing user base using Dictaphone machines. When they saw IBM and other manufacturers bringing out their speech systems, they panicked and announced their "continuous" system. Now, six months later, no product has actually been seen in the UK. I am sure that they are working on it.

However, work done in the UK shows that there may be a third important factor, known as "Phrase Technology". This is the term trade-marked by Shakespeare when their research showed that users do not actually speak continuously, but in phrases. This is half-way between the other two approaches, and "Phrase Technology" is gaining in popularity all the time.

At present, the School of Cognitive and Computing Science at Sussex University is furthering this research into Phrase Technology. They are attempting to analyse company correspondence corpora, to determine what phrases executives of a particular profession actually use. It could be that within a year an executive could run a software program that would analyse the correspondence of the previous two years and produce a phrase list that would enable direct dictation to the computer with 100% efficiency.

When it comes to recognition efficiency, the length of the utterance is of prime importance. With dalek speak systems, the recognition of small and frequently used words like "is" and "of" is much poorer than with longer, multi-syllabic words. With Phrase Technology many of the small words disappear within phrases, so the recognition efficiency is much greater.

With a continuous speech system, the whole rationale of analysis changes from analysing discrete packages and comparing these with a word or phrase database, to analysing continuous syllables and then building up words at the same time as doing sentence and contextual analysis.

WORD AND SENTENCE ANALYSIS VERSUS NO ANALYSIS

Context analysis is when the system scans the last few words and is able to distinguish between the use of words that sound the same but are spelt differently. For example, in the sentence, "The two boys went to the cinema", the system has to distinguish between "to", "too" and "two".

When Dragon brought out their first DOS system it had no contextual analysis. Their new Windows Dictate system has some analysis, which looks back over the last two words. The IBM system apparently looks back over three words.

The use of Phrase Technology to some degree eliminates the need for contextual analysis because the context is contained in the phrase.

The downside of contextual analysis is that it takes considerable processing power. This is very obvious with the IBM system, in which words have to be dictated into a separate dictation window and later transferred into the word processor or application. Not only that, but the contextual analysis takes so much power that the words appearing on the screen run about three words behind, which means that the system is not WYSIWYG. Users usually do not look at the screen at all when dictating, because it is distracting.

The Dragon system is WYSIWYG and, in the main, words appear immediately you say them. Sometimes there is a slight pause while the contextual analysis is done. This is generally eliminated if you are operating with a Pentium.

The Shakespeare system using Phrase Technology but no direct contextual analysis brings the phrases onto the screen instantly and is truly WYSIWYG.

Sentence analysis extends contextual analysis to take in complete grammatical and sense analysis over a whole sentence, even over a whole paragraph and eventually over an entire document.

It is my considered opinion that it will be at least another 10 years before continuous speech systems really are able to understand a user's natural voice and operate. I hope that I will be proved wrong and that the pace of technology will move quicker than that. Processors will have to become much more powerful. Contextual and sentence analysis by computers will need to come a long, long way from its very embryonic state at present.

The timescale that I predict for medium to very large vocabulary products, brought to market, is as follows:

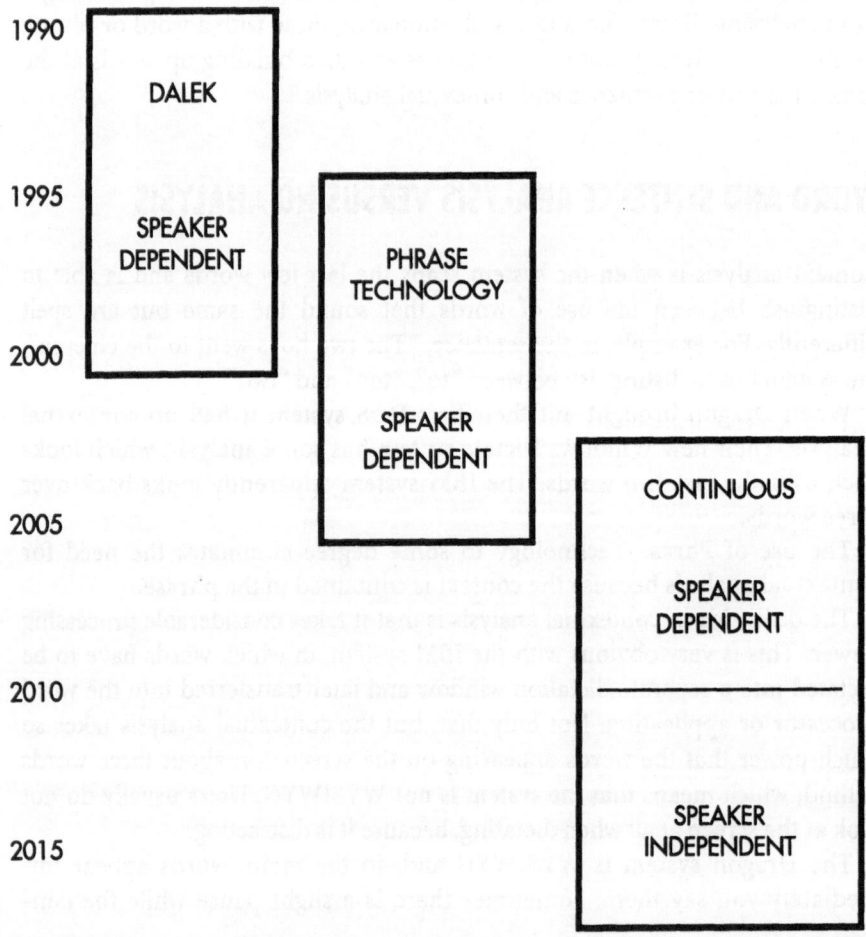

LARGE VERSUS SMALL VOCABULARIES

Traditionally, speech recognition had either very small vocabularies, such as 50 words, or large vocabularies, such as 30 000. The small vocabularies were used for command-and-control type applications and the larger vocabularies for dictation.

However, the speech industry has isolated various niche areas, where a variety of vocabulary sizes are required. Research work, done in the UK, has shown that many developers and system houses require multiple task-specific vocabularies.

These are vocabularies of up to 900 words that are relevant for a certain task and can thus be used for both command-and-control and dictation.

Table 3.2 gave a perspective on vocabulary sizes, but a better definition for research purposes is given in Table 7.1.

Table 7.1

LABEL	RANGE	TYPE
TINY	1–128	SINGLE
SMALL	129–1024	MULTIPLE
MEDIUM	1025–8196	MULTIPLE
LARGE	8197–32768	MULTIPLE
VERY LARGE	32769–65 536	SINGLE

The "tiny" vocabulary would only be up to 128 words and might as well all be in one vocabulary. This would be used for controlling a machine, for example, where all of the utterances would be commands and their scope would be very limited. Another example would be a speaker-independent system for interrogating accounts data over the telephone.

At the other end of the scale, the "very large" vocabulary might as well be a single vocabulary, because this would, no doubt, be used by an author or journalist reporting on a wide range of subjects. The main purpose would be to get large amounts of text into the word processor. There would be no reason for switching between a multiplicity of vocabularies.

However, all other sizes would certainly be more versatile by having multiple vocabularies. This is because they would be used both for entering text and for controlling the computer environment and applications.

BROAD VERSUS NARROW GRAMMAR

A broad grammar is the use of the English language in its normal form. A more narrow grammar would be to tell the system to expect a client code of the form NUMBER NUMBER LETTER, so that after hearing two numbers the system automatically listens only for a letter.

In the Dragon package, for example, you can go into command mode and say "File" and it will pop-up the file handling dialogue. At that point it does what Dragon calls "Tracking". Tracking keeps a note of what dialogue box the user is in, and arranges for only certain words to be active, which gives the user the choices available in that dialogue box. In operation this works well, although you have to say, "Command mode" first, which means that you are saying two commands instead of just one.

In the Dragon package you can add commands within the "dictate mode" large vocabulary that will operate straight into the dialogue, but this, unfortunately, does not reduce the grammar because all of the other 29 000 ordinary dictation words are still active. The chance of the system mis-recognizing a word is much higher, with the danger of it carrying out a command that you certainly did not intend.

In the Shakespeare packages a command within a vocabulary can automatically switch to a new vocabulary, which essentially reduces the grammar to what is available in the new vocabulary.

These points must be borne in mind when designing a voice recognition system.

REAL-TIME VERSUS OFF-LINE PROCESSING

When a system works in real time it processes the user's speech while it is happening: it is like a secretary taking shorthand.

Off-line processing is when the user's speech is taped onto a cassette and the computer is allowed to "think about it" overnight.

The Dragon and Shakespeare systems are real time. The IBM system is essentially real time, but because it does complex contextual analysis it is "real time minus one second". If you ran the IBM system on the fastest Pentium it may become real time again.

Many executives are still dictating their documents into a dictating machine and giving the cassette to their secretary to type up the report. You may well ask, "Why can't the secretary put the tape into the computer and have the computer type out the document from the recording?". The answer is that in fact this can be done, up to a point.

As I mentioned earlier, software programs have been devised by university teams that will take dictated text and produce a written document at about 93% efficiency. Anyone who has played with OCR (optical character recognition) will tell you that 93% is actually not efficient enough. To look through a document and correct 7% errors will take longer than just typing the document in the first place. Not only that, but you need a really powerful computer to do the analysis, and even then it may take six hours to process.

With more powerful computers being released each year there may come a point when an off-line system becomes viable. The dictation example may not be the first to be done off-line. Another, easier, example, which may be solved by developments in this technology, is data gathering.

A company may have a team of technicians who report data, which needs to be updated in a central database each day. They phone their results to the computer, which saves the recording as a "sound byte" on disk. Overnight, the computer analyses each sound byte, translating it into text and entering it into the database.

The technician may say, "Temperature sixteen". The computer hears the word "temperature" and can then analyse the next word, knowing that it will be a number. The efficiency, therefore, increases considerably because the vocabulary size, in this case, is reduced to a preset range of numbers.

It is my opinion that off-line speech processing for data collection will be another important niche area of development in the speech arena. I think that the off-line analysis of freeform dictation may take many more years of development before it becomes efficient enough to be used extensively. It may be that dictation of texts using "handheld" SpeechWriters supersedes such developments.

Microphone Technology

The starting point for all speech recognition is at the microphone. Whatever is spoken into the microphone goes down the wire to the computer system and is converted into commands or text. The better the microphone at picking up the person's voice, the better the final result of speech recognition.

There are six different designs of microphone available on the market:

1. *Appliance-mounted microphone*, such as that found in a cassette player or a microphone mounted in the case of a computer.
2. *Desktop microphone*, which is usually mounted on a stalk and positioned on the desk.

3. *Buttonhole microphone*, which is clipped to the user's lapel or tie.
4. *Headset microphone*, which is usually mounted on a headband with a small microphone arm extending the microphone head to the area of the lips.
5. *Radio microphone*, which is usually worn like a headset microphone but instead of having a cable going to the sound card has a radio or infrared transmitter.
6. *Powerful directional microphone*, which is mounted in the top corner of a room and is directionally tuned to pick up speech from a certain area of the room.

The first three are unsatisfactory for speech recognition purposes. The last three are listed in order of cost and availability.

APPLIANCE-MOUNTED MICROPHONE

This is the type of microphone that is mounted in a cassette player. Some computer manufacturers have tried to mount a small microphone inside the case of the computer.

Appliance-mounted microphones are usually £3 microphones, and simply are not powerful enough to be used for speech recognition.

DESKTOP MICROPHONE

This is the type of microphone that is mounted on a stalk and sits on the desk in front of the user. Although these microphones, in principle, can be used for speech recognition, they are not recommended. Users will naturally move their heads while dictating, and this gives variation of distance from the microphone. This variation is enough to upset the recognition process, so that words spoken begin to be mis-recognized. The user then has one choice to make it work: holding the head in a fixed position in front of the microphone. This is unnatural, causing stiff necks and discomfort.

Microphone technology is also a question of cost. The microphone heads that are installed in the long-stalked desktop mics that come with the cheaper sound systems probably cost between £5 and £10.

If you consider the microphones used, for example, in the BBC sound studios, which are also desktop microphones, you are talking about microphones costing between £200 and £400. Also, if you have ever gone into a radio station studio, you will know that any interviews are done in soundproofed rooms, with no background noise. This is very different to the noisy environment of an office, where background noise and general office hubbub play an important part in the design of an appropriate microphone for speech recognition.

BUTTONHOLE MICROPHONE

This is the type of microphone that is clipped to the lapel or tie. Again, these microphones are usually the cheap £3 microphones supplied with a computer or a sound system. They do not work because they are not powerful enough, and because they are not unidirectional. They not only pick up what the person is saying, but they also pick up every other sound in the room.

In 1993 Compaq supplied a buttonhole microphone with their machines and used the Microsoft Sound System, which included a speech recognition program to navigate the Windows desktop. This had a vocabulary of about 35 commands and 35 definable. It "sort of worked" when you tried hard, but most users dismissed it as a joke. One of the main problems with it was the microphone, which really was not adequate for voice recognition. As an additional note, the speech algorithm that Microsoft used was an early Dragon Windows system, and not Microsoft's own development.

One of the top executives from Microsoft was heard to comment, as late as May 1995, that the company did not feel that the speech industry was mature enough for them to enter it. He reckoned that it would be another four years before Microsoft brought out any speech products. If that is true then that policy may be attributed to the reaction that Microsoft got from their first attempted speech product. The product actually worked fine (within its very limited vocabulary size); its main failure was the microphone that manufacturers put out to run it.

HEADSET MICROPHONE

This is the type of microphone that is usually mounted on a headband with a small microphone arm extending the microphone head to the lips area. The reason why it is the preferred microphone is that it fits comfortably on the head and the wearer can forget its existence. When users move their head, the microphone will always be in exactly the correct place. That position is usually about three-quarters of an inch away from the side of the mouth.

All of the major speech recognition packages mentioned in this book are shipped with a headset microphone. The usual price of such a microphone would be about £75.

There are in fact, electrically, two types of headset microphone. A *dynamic* microphone is one that produces the electrical signal by the vibrations caused by the sound spoken by the user. It does not require any electricity to help it to produce the signal. Examples are the Audio Technica PRO8D dynamic headset microphone operating at 800 ohms, and the Shure SM10A dynamic headset microphone operating at 500–600 ohms.

A *condenser* microphone is one that operates with a working voltage across a 2000 resistor of between 1 and 6 volts. An example is the Primo condenser headset microphone. Some sound cards require a condenser microphone, because the signal produced by a dynamic microphone is too weak to drive the card properly.

Another example of a condenser microphone is the Shakespeare Pressure Gradient Microphone. This microphone has been specially designed for speech recognition so that it only picks up the nearest sound source. Thus, it filters out all extraneous background noise *before* sending the signal to the sound card.

Another feature of the headset microphone is that it can have a sound speaker as part of the ear assembly. This means that it can be used as a listening device if attached to the telephone. This really becomes important as computer/telephony integration becomes a reality.

RADIO MICROPHONE

This is the type of microphone that is usually worn as a headset microphone but instead of having a cable going to the sound card has a radio or infrared transmitter. At the sound card end there has to be a receiver, so that the transmitted signal can be picked up. These microphones are much more expensive, in the range of £300–600, depending on the specification. Because of the expense, these will only be used in a minority of cases by top executives who can afford them.

POWERFUL DIRECTIONAL MICROPHONE

This is the type of microphone that is mounted in the top corner of a room and is directionally tuned to pick up speech from a certain area of the room. This is your space age "invisible" microphone. It costs the earth and would probably only be used for demonstrating speech recognition technology to a meeting of the top European technocrats at the Albert Hall!

Sound Card Technology

The second link in the chain, from "user" to "text on the screen of the computer" is the sound card. When someone speaks an utterance into the microphone, that sound vibration is converted into an analogue signal, which goes down the wire to the sound card. An analogue signal is defined as "a smoothly varying value of voltage or current, which often represents a measured physical quality". In this case the sound waves, which are sinusoidal, are converted to a fluctuating electrical current that matches the original sinusoidal pattern.

When this fluctuating electrical current arrives at the sound card, the first job that the sound card does is to change the analogue signal into a digital signal. The "chip" component on the sound card that does this is called an analogue–digital converter or A-D converter for short. The net result is that the sinusoidal wave ends up as a 011110001100111 digital code.

If you look at a Creative Labs Sound Blaster SB-16 card you will find that it has an A-D converter chip and a D-A converter chip. The card has the capability, for example, of recording your voice as a digital file on the hard disk and then playing it back through the loudspeaker output port of the card. The playback system uses the D-A converter chip to do this. In the same way, the card can read the digitally recorded tunes from a music CD and play these while you are doing your word processing.

Once the utterance has been converted into digital code it has to be analysed by the speech system to translate it into words or commands. This is done in three stages:

1. The digital signal is cleaned up, any background noise is removed and the end of the utterance is determined. This is called the *pre-processing* stage.
2. The final digital representation of the utterance is compared with the database of words (called the speech pattern) to find words (phrases or commands) that match this digital representation. This is the *processing* stage.
3. The results of this comparison are passed to the application program, which then uses these results either to operate a command or to display the word or phrase within the word processor or other application. This is known as the *post-processing* stage.

The Creative Labs Sound Blaster AWE32 card is a much more powerful and expensive card, which has a digital signal processing (DSP) chip, as well as the A-D and D-A converter chips. The DSP chip has the capability of doing the pre-processing stage on the card, before the results are passed to the CPU for the next stage.

With the SB16 card the pre-processing stage has to be done by the program itself in the CPU. This puts more load on the CPU, which is why speech programs actually work better with an AWE32 card when you are running it on a 486 33 MHz computer. The results at 486 66 MHz are marginally better, and when you run the program on a Pentium computer the card type makes no difference to the speech recognition speed. Note, however, that the AWE32 card does have other facilities that may be required.

The processing stage is done in the CPU by a program that has been written by the manufacturer whose speech algorithm you are using. This is normally a .DLL file such as DRAGON.DLL. The method that this .DLL program uses to search for the correct word in the speech pattern is covered in the following two sections.

The post-processing stage is done in the CPU by a program written by the package producers. This is normally an .EXE file, such as SPEECH.EXE in the case of Shakespeare's products.

The Creative Labs sound cards and the Media Vision sound cards are all Microsoft Sound System compatible. What that means is that they will run all of the programs in the Microsoft Sound System. This includes playing music CDs, recording a user's sound bytes, and playing back sound bytes that have been saved on hard disk in various formats.

There are a plethora of other sound cards coming onto the market from various manufacturers. In the main, these are Microsoft Sound System and Sound Blaster compatible, in as much as the speech systems will work with them.

A new type of card, called a PCMCIA sound card, is also being brought to the market. This card looks like a thick credit card and fits into a special slot in the newer computers now being manufactured. PCMCIA cards are also, in the main, Microsoft Sound System and Sound Blaster compatible.

The IBM speech card and the IBM PCMCIA card (which is normally sold only with the speech system) are proprietary cards. They each have a DSP chip. They are not Microsoft Sound System compatible; they can only be used with IBM speech products.

The Techmar ACPA card is supported by Dragon (both DOS and Windows products) and by Shakespeare (Windows products only). The card has a DSP chip on board but is not Microsoft Sound System compatible.

The normal choice for an executive buying a non-IBM speech system is a Sound Blaster card. This gives the speech recognition facilities but also gives the user access to the Microsoft Sound System facilities. It is also very much cheaper than an ACPA card.

The ALPS Sound Tower is a proprietary sound card that fits on the parallel port of the computer and thus does not use up a slot inside the computer. It has a DSP chip in the tower. It is sold only as a part of the ALPS speech system. It is not Microsoft Sound System compatible and has no other function than to support the speech recognition system.

Finally, a note on where the industry will move on sound cards over the next five years. Intel will be a major manufacturer of motherboards during this period. They plan to put facilities like sound, network and modem on their motherboards, so there will be no necessity to have plug-in cards. The sound part will probably not include a DSP chip, so all of the sound processing will need to be done in the CPU. This will be no problem, because the Pentium P5, P6 and future P7 will be able to handle that processing, with no degradation to ordinary processing speed.

As for other manufacturers and notebook manufacturers, they may follow Intel's lead in this matter but will certainly change over to the PCMCIA type cards rather than the larger plug-in cards that go in the box.

Database Searching and Template Matching

In this and the next section I will try to explain, in the simplest way, the second stage of the sound analysis, the processing stage. Here, the digital representation of the utterance is used to search the speech pattern for the best matches.

Two main types of search algorithms are used. Most speech manufacturers use the neural network approach. However, the earlier method for doing the searching was called *template matching*. This search algorithm is used, for example, in the ALPS products. The underlying speech algorithm in this case was written by an American company called Scott.

Template matching technology works in a unique way. The digital representation of the utterance in template matching is called a *token*. This token is then compared to the templates in the currently active vocabulary. The template that most closely matches the token is then chosen as the word that the user uttered. There is a difference between templates and tokens: the token is a representation of what the user actually said, whereas the templates contain different information. The templates try to highlight the differences between the different words.

So, for example, if you have only one word in the vocabulary starting with the letters "th", such as "though", then the template for "though" may contain only the sounds "th". This is done to highlight the differences between the words so that the algorithm can most easily distinguish between them.

When a word is trained, all of the templates in the vocabulary are updated, not just the word trained. This is because information about any one word is useful in highlighting the differences between all words in the system.

Speech Recognition Using Neural Networks

The second method of searching the user's speech pattern for the correct word uses a statistical technique that was originally developed by Andrei Markov (1852–1922), a Russian mathematician. Markov did important work in probability theory and, although this work is highly mathematical, the principle can be explained by the use of a simple diagram known as a *neural network*. It is known as a "neural" network because it matches how scientists believe the brain and nervous system operate (Fig. 7.1).

$$(2*3)+(5*7)+(1*4)=45 \qquad (6*2)+(8*7)+(3*4)=80$$

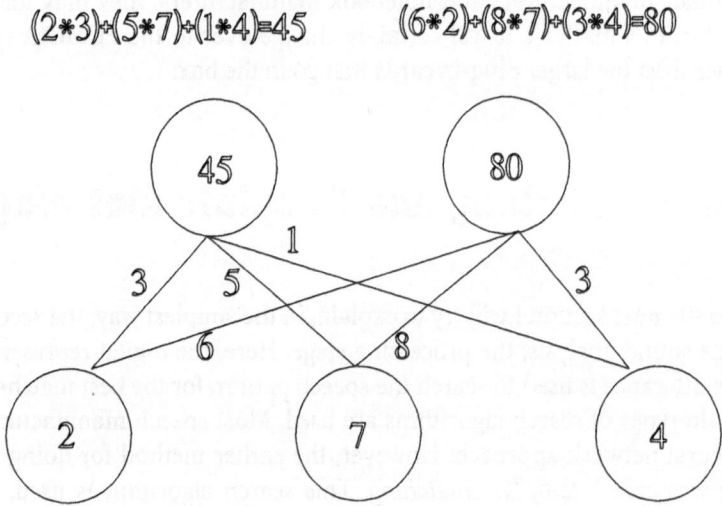

In Fig. 7.1, the input is weighted, and each path through the network also has a weighting. These weightings are then multiplied together, which then gives a final score on the next layer of circles. This tells the system which circle (i.e. word) to choose. Figure 7.1 shows only one layer, but with a speech system the layers are several deep and depend on other exceptions as well. The full technique is known as a *hidden Markov model.*

The parlance used in the speech industry to explain this is that the hidden Markov model is a collection of states and transitions (i.e. paths) between these states. Each transition is marked with three things:

1. The probability with which that transition is taken.
2. An output value.
3. The probability that the output value is emitted when the transition is taken.

These hidden Markov models learn to correspond to digital representations of the wave forms that are the user's voice pattern. The hidden Markov model can thus learn all the time, and become more accurate as time goes on.

The Use of Artificial Intelligence in Speech Systems

Because AI is a relatively young science there still seems to be some argument as to what it actually is, or whether it even exists as a field in its own right. There are people who believe that AI is just a glorified subfield of computer science!

However, on reading various definitions of AI, it seems that most researchers would agree that AI is concerned with analysing "intelligent" behaviours and modelling these on computers. For example, Elaine Rich and Kevin Knight define AI in the following way:

> *"Artificial Intelligence is the study of how to make computers do things which at the moment people do better."* (Artificial Intelligence, *2nd edn, 1991, McGraw-Hill, New York, p. 3)*

The *Dictionary of Artificial Intelligence* gives a similar definition:

> *"...artificial intelligence or AI, n. the field of computer science that seeks to understand and implement computer-based technology that can simulate characteristics of human intelligence."* (Smith, 1990, p. 22)

Currently humans are much better at understanding other humans than computers are. What is more, no speech recognition algorithm really makes intelligent sense of the context in which the person is speaking. Speech recognition algorithms have come a long way, but for them really to start understanding the everyday, ever changing language that we speak, they must be able to make more intelligent use of the context in which the user is speaking, and have some knowledge about the subject that the person is speaking about. This is where research into artificial intelligence and speech recognition go hand in hand.

There are several levels at which we can analyse speech being spoken into the microphone:

- *Phonetic level analysis* is where the individual sounds that make up a word are analysed. For example, the *k* as in "cat", as an opening phoneme (individual sound) can be analysed. The next phoneme following the *k* can only be from a narrow group of vowel-type sounds, for example the *a* of "cat", the *e* of "kestrel", the *i* of "kite", the *o* of "cot" or the *u* of "cut", or a limited number of consonant-type sounds, such as the *l* of "clatter" or the *r* of "credit". Each one of these "follow-on" sounds will have a probability score of occurring according to the language or dialect being spoken.

- *Word level analysis* is where the whole word is taken into consideration, working backwards from the sounds that make up that word. In the main, that should give a unique word spelling, with the exception of homonyms, such as "to", "too" and "two".
- *Meaning level analysis* is where the meaning of a word can be different even though it is spelt the same, for example, kite meaning either a bird, a child's flying toy or a cheque.
- *Phrase level analysis* is where combinations of words can again have different meanings to the original words, such as "iron curtain".
- *Sentence level analysis* is where the occurrence of a wrong word can be isolated because it does not fit into the overall meaning of the sentence within the subject matter being discussed.

The discontinuous (dalek) speech algorithms being used in speech recognition programs today only take in the crude use of a couple of these analyses. The algorithms of tomorrow, which will cater fully for continuous speech, will need to take into consideration all of these different analyses.

Research and Development in Speech: Series Editor's Notes

We have so far assumed the availability of systems incorporating a database of speech patterns, deriving suggested meanings by making matches. Our concentration has been on the recognition of commands.

Humans use language for more than commands. This has been recognized in the development of speech-driven word processing systems, a computerized extension of Dictaphones. For the university academic, there is the temptation to deliver the lecture to the computer screen, and invite the student to send comments and questions by electronic mail.

SPOKEN QUERIES TO DATABASES

We also use speech and language to ask questions. Given that computers are used as repositories of vast stores of information, we would like to be able to search and retrieve through the use of speech.

The necessary background research has been carried out in natural language processing, although this has not as yet been linked to widely available speech-driven personal computers. With the advent of affordable mass storage and high speed retrieval systems, including systems based on parallel architectures, the way is open for major developments.

Work has been done over the past 20 years in the field of natural language querying of databases. Questions in English, or some other "natural language", have been converted into queries, often using logic and formalisms such as definite clause grammars. There is a long research tradition at the text level, which should be translatable into practical speech-activated products. The work of Warren and Pereira in Edinburgh in the early 1980s, and speech and language processing work done by SRI and Logica in Cambridge in the mid- to late 1980s showed how logic could link language and databases. There was, however, a problem in securing active interest from major business users. The time may have come for commercial exploitation.

SPEECH-DRIVEN WORKSTATIONS

In 1983 speech-activated systems were a research objective rather than a business reality. The largest project in the British Government's Alvey Programme of Research and Development in Advanced Information Technology was the speech-driven workstation, running on the innovative and highly parallel FLAGSHIP computer. The partners included ICL, Plessey, Imperial College, Manchester University, Edinburgh University and Loughborough University. The ambitious project sought to take advantage of highly parallel computer architecture to produce acceptable response times in speech processing, sufficient to drive a word processor. Many of the components of the project required research breakthroughs. The past decade has seen changes in ownership of the companies concerned, which has jeopardized the continuity of research and development.

The Alvey Programme researcher teams were more ambitious in their research, seeking to process continuous speech, which required stages of signal processing, pattern recognition and computational linguistics.

SPEECH-DRIVEN BUSINESS ENGLISH

Today's commercial products are more modest, but the technology works. As the author has suggested, we can expect further advances over the coming years. The work of McPherson and Metzger with Sussex University demonstrates the pragmatic power of "phrase speak". This is language in practical use, as a tool of immense potential.

Given the explosive expansion of the use of "business English" as the *de facto* international language, accelerated by the end of the Cold War and the rise of the "tiger economies" of the Far East, fascinating new possibilities arise. We could envisage the production of a "Business English Phrase Book", containing the components for well-formed business letters and official documents. This could be linked with sets of speech patterns from speakers in the different geographical and ethnic contexts, which can then be tailored to the needs of individual users. We must recall that users of business English may have learned American or Australian, rather than British, English. The commands to be executed by the computer will be the same, though the sounds made by the user will vary considerably.

This is the basis for a Millennium Project.

Environmental Changes

8

Introduction

In this chapter we are going to describe some of the environmental aspects that we may expect from the introduction of speech recognition into the workplace. These topics are as follows:

- Medical aspects of speech recognition
- Workplace reorganization

Medical Aspects of Speech Recognition

Most companies, both large and small, are becoming computerized. Work for very many people consists of turning on the screen in the morning and sitting at the keyboard all day. The effects of this lifestyle (or should we say workstyle) on the body can only be detrimental over a long period of time.

To cap it all, many of these workers then go home and watch television each night.

The effects on the eyes have been documented, and European law now insists that all staff who use a VDU should have regular eye tests. Radiation levels of screens have been reduced over the past 10 years, and this area does seem to be getting constant review to improve the lot of staff members.

The effects of typing on a keyboard have yet to be accepted as a recognized industrial injury. Repetitive strain injury (RSI) is the umbrella term for disorders with various symptoms, including swelling and chronic pain in the hand, similar symptoms in the arms and shoulders, and the complete seizure of the hands and fingers. The Health and Safety Executive, the government watchdog, avoids the term RSI, because it implies that these problems are only caused by repetition, and refers to any such ailments as "upper limb disorders".

In 1994 a journalist with the Reuters news agency brought a case against the company on the basis that his work conditions using computer keyboards were responsible for injuries to his upper limbs. In the event, the journalist lost the case because the judge ruled that his injuries, although genuine, had been caused by personal stress rather than by his computer keyboard.

In previous High Court rulings, judges have accepted the existence of RSI. The leader of the GMB union in the UK said, in 1994, that his union had recovered more than £1 million in compensation for RSI suffers since 1987. Referring to the case mentioned above, he said, "Does the judge think that companies like Slazenger, Birds Eye, Findus and KP Foods have paid compensation to our members because of a figment of their imagination?".

Since this time many more RSI cases have gone in favour of the RSI sufferer and it has become accepted that there is a link between RSI and keyboards. In America there have now been thousands of lawsuits filed against computer manufacturers by individuals claiming to have been injured through using keyboards.

To counteract this legal time bomb, both Compaq and Microsoft are now putting warning notices on all of their keyboards. I am sure that all other manufacturers will follow their lead.

Speech recognition products, as outlined in this book, will go a long way towards alleviating these problems. As the number of lawsuits increases, investment in speech technology will increase to prevent very costly compensation claims.

Workplace Reorganization

The one question that is asked many times by executives who are thinking of buying a SpeechWriter is, "doesn't background noise interfere with the operation of the SpeechWriter?". The answer, of course, is that it does affect the operation to a small degree but this interference can be minimized and even eliminated altogether. All of the speech programs have built-in background noise elimination routines, which operate many times a second. Also, the choice of microphone is paramount. A pressure gradient headset microphone will eliminate almost all distant noises, before the processing of the utterance even begins.

If you are training the system to your voice, then doing so in a reasonably quiet room does aid the training process because the speech pattern is without extraneous sounds mingled with your rendition of the word or phrase. It must be said that if the system is set to learn all the time, as in the IBM and Dragon systems, that can have an adverse effect on its efficiency.

In the case of the Dragon product, after the training period has been implemented, this continual learning process can be turned off, which can stabilize the system.

If the speech product is fairly stable, as in the case of the Shakespeare products, which only learn when you are training the phrase, then the speech recognition efficiency will not be affected by background noise at all.

So, how does this data affect the reorganization of the office environment? In general, authors, top executives who are doing "wide" reports and documents, and journalists would benefit from being in their own office, where the background noise is kept to a minimum. They would all be using large or very large vocabulary systems. Other staff, who are doing more repetitive work and thus are using a more stable product, would be fine in an open-plan office.

When telephones were first introduced, the larger corporations in open-plan offices built little cubicles, so that telephone users would not disturb each other. Gradually over the years, these cubicles and "separators" have disappeared, and truly open-plan offices are now found. Nobody seems to mind about telephoning in front of other staff members, and usually conversations are lost in the general hubbub of the office.

I am sure that when speech activation is first introduced in volume to large open-plan offices there will be a clamour for resurrecting the partitions. This will mostly be because of embarrassment and ineptitude, rather than because of interference. Three months down the road, staff will gaily talk to their PCs without thinking twice if anyone is listening.

Environmental Changes: Series Editor's Notes

USES

What is the technology for?

- Is it to enhance the effectiveness of individuals, or to increase efficiency by reducing the number of staff employed?
- Is it another way of taking a fresh look at communication?

ABUSES

It is becoming apparent that new technology is not always beneficial.

- Are there cases where the technology has been clearly *dis*abling rather than *en*abling?
- How much do we really understand about RSI?
- How serious are companies in adhering to the terms of European Union health and safety directives?

CHANGE

Some organizational issues are physical, concerned with the pragmatics of microphone use in offices, and the practical means of providing adequate training. Improved microphones reduce the need for soundproofing and specialist training, but leave other questions unresolved.

- How should speech technology be introduced into the workplace?
- Do people benefit from sharing the same working space, rather than being allocated separate cubicles?
- Is human interaction restricted by the individual use of microphones and speech activation?
- Do we have enough experience to draw conclusions?

CRITICAL SUCCESS FACTORS

What are the preconditions for successful use of speech-driven technology?

- Do we need a product champion inside the user organization, or can the change be driven purely from outside?
- Who needs to know what?
- Who typically knows what?

INVESTMENT

What is the real scale of investment required?

- How does it produce payback?
- Are there cultural as well as financial benefits?
- Who has to take what decisions?

NEW TECHNOLOGY, OLD QUESTIONS

Many of the questions raised by novel speech technology are not new. Some are addressed in companion volumes in the *Executive Guide* series, such as *Executive Guide to Preventing Information Technology Disasters* and *Executive Guide to Business Success through Human-Centred Systems.*

Conclusions

9

In this chapter I am going to try to draw some conclusions from the wealth of data presented.

The object of the book was to give you, the executive, the information you require to evaluate whether, and how, you might implement this new speech technology in your company.

This period in time is the beginning of a new era in the operation of computers: the point in history when users started to talk to their machines.

If you go back five years, when Windows first appeared, most computer users at the time were very sceptical about this new Windows technology, and even more sceptical about using this new gadget called a mouse. Now, the mouse is completely accepted as complementing the keyboard in the operation of the computer. Take away the mouse from today's user and basically he won't be able to operate his computer. Not many users know the equivalent key combinations to operate solely by the keyboard.

Enter speech, and the same sort of resistance to the "new" will be met. Five years hence and speech will be completely accepted as the norm.

If you talk to users who have already taken on this technology, they will tell you that they could not really do without speech. It complements the other two entry methods. Users who are able bodied certainly still use the mouse, and quite often use the keyboard to some extent, for those things that a keyboard is really good at, but in the main they use speech.

For users who have disabilities, speech is a new lease of life. One of the users whom I have had the privilege to work with, in setting up his speech system, is a successful architect who contracted polio and is now paralysed from the neck down. Despite his disability, he leads a remarkably normal life, and, with the power of speech, is now designing full colour advertising campaigns, including drawing all the pictures. You have really got to see it to believe it.

So, the first conclusion is to say to you, the executive, now is the time to get to grips with this technology. It is quite amusing for me to be saying this, because it took at least three years before I was convinced about Windows. Looking back, basically I was stupid and stubborn not to have used its facilities from the beginning.

Secondly, it doesn't cost an arm and a leg to get on the bandwagon. You can buy one of the medium vocabulary packages for less than £400. Get your hands dirty – or should we be saying, as we are cutting down on keyboarding, give your mouth a morsel? Only by working with the technology do you begin to realize the power that it gives you. Just think you – yes, you – will be talking to a machine. You will be making history.

Thirdly, once you have some inside knowledge of the technology, you will be able to make a more educated plan to implement speech in your company. There are areas that will spring to mind. It may be that you will speech activate your accounts before you give your MD a dictating facility. Your production line may have very soiled keyboards, which could be replaced by speech, leaving your operators with their hands free.

Fourthly, your speech dealer will most likely give you an upgrade path, so that if you want to upgrade your medium vocabulary speech system to a large vocabulary system, it will be possible to do so.

Finally, you should work with your dealer to get news of all the latest offerings from the speech manufacturers. Like the rest of the computer industry, the pace of speech developments goes at ever increasing speed. The information in this book, by the time you buy it, will probably be out of date. It is fortunate that the underlying principles do not change too rapidly.

I have in this book been very specific in describing the principles behind speech activation and the packages that have resulted from the underlying speech technology. I trust that you have also found the broader view, given by the Series Editor's Notes, to have been thought provoking as well as very interesting.

It only remains for me to wish you well on this new exciting path of "talking to your computer".

Appendix: Messages for Executives

In the Series Editor's Introduction we posed some questions, to which we can now offer answers, which should lead to action.

Why Is Speech Technology Important?

After centuries of imaginative fiction and decades of scientific endeavour, speech technology is an affordable working reality. The keyboard may come to be seen as a temporary aberration, a relic of the time when computing was for the elite few.

Speech is a defining characteristic of what it is to be human: with speech-driven computing we see the prospect of wider access to current applications of computers, and a widening of the range of applications. With speech-driven computers, speech becomes action.

Major companies are now jockeying for position, seeking to ensure that they can secure the benefits of speech activation for their own competitive advantage. There have been false starts, with excessive promises and inadequate technology. We have learned from experience that the most sophisticated software can be made to appear inadequate if it is accompanied by a low quality microphone, and vice versa.

Speech technology is not the equivalent of an enhanced operating system, or a new faster computer chip. It offers the prospect of a qualitative change in the way in which computers are used, without obliging users to change their choice of current software applications, or imposing major costs in terms of hardware. It is available today, running with industry standard hardware and software.

Speech linked to computers offers the prospect of resolution of age-old problems of communication. For example, people working in a common business area may speak different natural languages. With matched "phrase speak" systems they will be able to undertake business dialogue. Those with a disability that has prevented them from using the keyboard should have the opportunity of demonstrating their capability: using a different interface system to software applications they will produce output indistinguishable from that of "able-bodied" users. With the rapidly falling cost of hardware and software, both of which have achieved commodity status, the cost of entry into business computing for the previously non-computer literate is distinctly affordable. Already we see primary schools that are better equipped than commercial companies, thanks to the rapid generational change in microprocessors. The next generation could be speaking to computers as if it were the most natural thing to do.

Speech technology does not remove the need for programming, but casts it in a new light. When we decide that a particular utterance should be taken as requesting a stated form of action, we are formulating a line in a program. When we identify a particular pattern of speech acts that should be interpreted in a given way, we are starting to use rules. We begin to see that the separate activities of management and programming begin to converge.

Why Is Speech Technology Important for Busy Executives Today?

Busy executives can no longer delegate all work concerned with computers to technical colleagues. Computers are on every desk, but the keyboard and screen can seem obstacles to the majority of managers, who have not previously been computer enthusiasts, and have had little opportunity for training.

It should be possible to talk to the computer, and drive standard applications such as word processors, organizers and spreadsheets, as well as in-house bespoke systems. The computer responds to clear speaking and clear thinking: it obliges the manager to think before speaking. Confused utterances by the manager will lead to confused actions from the computer system.

Given that managers are converging on common standards with respect to hardware and software, and low cost starter speech activation systems are available to operate alongside conventional keyboard and mouse operation, the argument for experimental use by the innovative, ambitious executive is hard to resist.

How Will Speech Technology Affect the Executive and the Organization?

Who is the executive, and who makes up the organization?

There has been an assumption that one group of people, known as executives, is responsible for making decisions to be carried out by another group. The executive has been accustomed to dictating a letter to a secretary, and later approving a draft before signing the finished item.

If the executive is able to dictate the letter to the computer, the role of the secretary may change. It may be, of course, that the secretary is better at dictating business letters, and has a deeper understanding of how the business is organized and supported by the computer, in which case it is the role of the executive that is in question. It may be that the letter, indeed the whole correspondence, becomes superfluous, in which case the roles of all members of the organization require review.

Speech technology forces issues of business process re-engineering. The conventional tasks can now be performed by new means, new tasks become possible, and the structure of the organization may have to change as a result.

The busy executive is probably now working in an organization that has undergone structural change. The centrally controlled hierarchy has been replaced by a flatter networking set of relationships, with less secretarial and administrative support available. Planning ahead is difficult amid turbulent change.

One justification for considering speech technology is that it forces the realization that the organization could operate differently, that long-held assumptions may no longer apply. It is better to explore and choose a new direction than to be surprised and obliged to change. Executives who do not take a serious interest in speech technology may discover too late that they have become surplus to requirements. Indeed, speech technology could be a valuable tool for management development, obliging participants to join an activity where at present all are novices.

How Can Speech Technology Offer Competitive Advantage?

The critical issue with the use of speech in business is the action that follows. This point applies whether or not technology is used, and to that extent the technology drops out of consideration as a separate item.

Organizations are most effective if the members share a common language, operate within a common culture, and have common commitments to action following from words. Where there is trust and mutual confidence, the quality of decision making and policy delivery is enhanced. Within such an organization, if there is a common network infrastructure, with technical support for the range of software application tools that enhance management creative activity, then speech activation is likely to offer considerable competitive advantage.

What Are the Next Steps?

All organizations that wish to operate in the next century need to be gaining experience of the oldest human technology, speech, linked to the latest industry standard hardware and software.

As described earlier, a number of affordable commercial systems are now available, with dealers happy to demonstrate their wares. It is important to avoid the trap of watching a single demonstration, taking a passive approach to speech activation. It is well worth "playing with" a speech-driven computer system as if it were simply a toy, as long as you then put it to the test of a small task relevant to your organization's needs. The meaning of the technology will be seen in its use.

There follow some suggested small-scale projects, using the systems described in the book, that would enable the busy executive to break the ice, and gain the confidence that only comes from experience.

- In every management job there are standard form letters that have to be sent, with only names and addresses changed. Choose one, and use speech input to send it to five different people.
- Write down the twenty key phrases used in your specialist area, and the actions that should follow from their use. What you have produced can be seen as either a phrase book or a program.

- Prepare a case for your manager, identifying a business task that could usefully be performed with the assistance of speech technology; offer to give a presentation of your results to senior colleagues.

Within your organization you will need to identify a small group of people, ideally drawn from different specialisms, who are interested in working together and sharing their experiences.

Many companies and hard-pressed organizations will lack the confidence and technical competence to venture alone into a new technical field. This is where human networking delivers benefits, working with others with whom you share a conversation.

At this stage the use of speech technology is new to all, and there have been few published accounts on which to build. As with computer supported cooperative working and multimedia, commercial development has followed hard on the heels of research without proper time for publication and debate.

Speech is different in a radical way: it is something almost all of us do, and have done since infancy. The challenge is to bring our long experience of speech to our use of new technology, rather than the other way round.

It's good to talk....

Just say the word....

My word is my bond....

In the beginning was the Word....

Index